# GOVERNANCE FOR THE HUMANS
## Designing Public Policy in India

# Governance for the Humans

## Designing Public Policy in India

### R.N. GUPTA
IAS (Retd.)

GOVERNANCE FOR THE HUMANS
Designing Public Policy in India
R.N. Gupta

© R.N. Gupta 2016

First Published 2016

ISBN 978-93-83723-16-4

*Published by*
**LG PUBLISHERS DISTRIBUTORS**
49, Street No. 14, Pratap Nagar,
Mayur Vihar Phase I, Delhi 110091
Email: lgpdist@gmail.com

*In Association with*
**INSTITUTE FOR DEVELOPMENT & COMMUNICATION**
Sector 38A, Chandigarh 160 014
Phones: 0172-262 5941, 466 0038
idcindia@idcindia.org, www.idcindia.org

*Designed by*
Limited Colors, Delhi 110 092

*Printed at*
Saurabh Printers Pvt. Ltd., Greater Noida

*To*

*my wife Vijaya*

*and*
*grand children*
*Soumya, Kartik, Adit and Dhruv*

# Contents

*Preface: On a Note of Personal Explanation*     ix

*Introduction: Designing 'Human-Centred' Regulations*     1

1. Donation of Organs: Framework of a Human Policy     13

2. Female Foeticide: Even Inhuman Acts need Human Rules     23

3. Road Safety: Regulatory 'Nudges' for Human Drivers     36

4. Rules for Human Smokers and Drinkers     50

5. Income Tax Law: Changing the Default Settings     61

6. Crime Control: Guarding the Guardians     72

7. Bureaucracy: Playing the Game of Honesty     85

8. Dedicated Bureaucracy: The Carrot or the Stick?     95

9. Performance Pay for the Bureaucracy     104

10. Indian Bureaucracy: Thinking Outside the Box     110

11. Labour Laws: The Devil's in the Detail     114

12. Public Services: Moral Hazard of Self Certification     123

13. Ease of Doing Business: Licence-Permit Raj     130

14. Governance: By Experts or Algorithms?     134

15. Redesigning Rules of the Game: From Noise to Cooperation     143

*Index*     151

# Preface
## On a Note of Personal Explanation

While cutting my teeth on the first Secretariat assignment with the Punjab government, I was advised by a senior colleague that various policy proposals, 'files' and 'cases' should be processed, examined and analysed keeping in mind three basic dimensions—administrative, legal and financial. In due course, officials also need to acquire the outlook and bias of the specialised agency or department they work for, as I discovered on my subsequent posting as Under Secretary in a Ministry of the Government of India. I had barely settled down to the routine of a somewhat furious examination of various proposals from the aforesaid perspectives when I was told that I must also examine them from the 'foreign aid' angle; that was the division of the Ministry I was assigned to. A power project is viewed very differently by the power utility and the environmental control agency, not to speak of the people affected. Similarly, the outlook of the Police Department and the Ministry of Justice on juvenile crime is likely to be very different. Then there is the political dimension which the middle level bureaucrats are not expected to worry about. These perspectives and reference points may be the bread and butter of bureaucratic efficiency but do not seem very relevant for policy outcomes. Bureaucrats and policy makers would therefore do well to also take into consideration the often neglected fifth dimension, of behaviour and how human beings actually behave rather than how they should; after all, it is for them that the government policies and programmes are designed.

Though research on the relevance of a behavioural or behaviourally informed approach was initiated by Kahneman and Tversky[1] in the 1970s, there has been a surge of public curiosity and interest after the publication of *Nudge*[2] in 2008. I happened to read the review in *The Economist*, ordered the same from Amazon (the book was not available in India then) and was well and truly bitten by the bug. Malcolm Gladwell in his fascinating book *The Tipping Point* mentions three rules for ideas and products to take off and become 'social epidemics' – the law of the few, the stickiness factor and the power of context[3]. The last of these factors, context, did play a role in getting me hooked. I happened at that time to be associated with a state government Commission on governance reforms. We were not very comfortable in dressing up the traditional and somewhat tired tools and instruments—resources, staff, reorganisation, restructuring—as reforms and were desperately searching for innovative solutions. I don't mind confessing, however, that I failed to turn my 'infection' into an 'epidemic'. The reason was again another of Gladwell's rules, the law of the few; I was, to use his words, neither a 'maven' nor 'connector' nor even a 'salesman'.

Nudge is the commonly used term now to denote a behavioural perspective, but, as will be seen later, it is somewhat inadequate to describe its range and scope. Einstein had looked, without much success, for a unifying theory or principle for the four major forces in the physical world—gravitation, electo-magnetism and weak and strong nuclear forces. I don't know whether the search is over now with the string theory but in my view a behavioural approach is the integrator, the 'theory of everything' for the world of public governance. The beauty is that once you discover the behavioural tree, there is plenty of low hanging fruit available.

It needs to be emphasized that a behavioural or behaviourally informed perspective is very different from the discredited school of behaviourism with which it has only a semantic association. Behaviourism was founded by John B. Watson and was popular from 1920's to 1960s; according to this school, human beings do not have any innate propensities, talents or traits, and behaviour is a product of nurture, not nature. It probably matters little what the main springs of behaviour are—genetics, evolutionary psychology and hunter-gatherer heritage or physical and social environment; we now know, as Matt Ridley shows, that both nature and nurture matter in shaping behaviour[4].

A number of countries have incorporated this approach in the making of public policy and have set up dedicated agencies to adopt and propagate this perspective in the making of public policy and designing rules and regulations. The UK government took the lead by setting up a Behavioural Insights Team known as the 'Nudge Unit'. Cass R. Sunstein, the co-author of *Nudge* was the head of the OIRA (Office of Information and Regulatory Affairs) in the US Federal Government and introduced this bias in the design of regulations and their simplification. The effectiveness of mild interventions such as 'nudges' and 'default rules' specifically, and a behaviour based approach generally, has been demonstrated in many countries in areas such as taxes and donation of organs (UK), pensions (Sweden), and redesigning and simplification of regulations, statutes and processes as well as school education (USA). India's 'regulatory czars', however, continue to persist with their pathetic faith in tough mandates and bans, and are fond of designing rules as 'moral imperatives'. This needs to change if we wish to avoid governance failure, a common experience with most of the public policies and programmes.

The book is in a way an extension of *Governance Unbound: Public Services, Players and Rules of the Game* published in 2014, but covers a number of new areas (road safety, female foeticide, smoking, bureaucracy). Some of the chapters extend the arguments presented earlier (crime, labour laws). I was also able during this interregnum to indulge in thought experiments, through 'what if' scenarios, during discussions with professionals and others interested in improving governance, even though, as mentioned above, they were not really enthused by the new perspective. I have also tried to make this book more reader friendly; it is meant to be a sort of DIY (Do It Yourself) or rather TIY (Think It Yourself) kit for public officials and others responsible for and interested in designing public policy and the rules of the game.

## Endnotes

1 Kahneman and Tversky's two path breaking articles on Heuristics and Biases (1974) and Prospect Theory (1983).
2 Thaler, Richard H. and Sunstein, Cass R. (2008), *Nudge: Improving Decisions About Health, Wealth, and Happiness*, Yale University Press, New Haven, USA.
3 Gladwell, Malcolm, 2000/2010, T*he Tipping Point: How Little Things Can Make a Big Difference*, Abacus.
4 Ridley, Matt (2003), *Nature via Nurture*, Fourth Estate, UK.

# Introduction
## Designing 'Human-Centred' Regulations

"In the present crisis, government is not a solution to our problem; government is the problem": the remark made by Ronald Reagan during his inaugural address as President of the USA became the mantra for a new governance paradigm in the 1980s. The NPM (New Public Management) which replaced the interventionist welfare state, however, may only end up throwing out the baby with the bath water. Business management is concerned with the production and sale of material and (increasingly) intangible products, is obsessed with profits and it is, therefore, somewhat difficult to transplant its culture, mores and ethos into the complex area of governance of humans. And arm's length governance can only take us so far; remember the desperate pleas for state intervention following the collapse of different markets—savings and loans in the USA in 1980s, the dot com bust in the 1990s and investment and banking crisis in 2008.

## Myth of minimum government

In India, despite the freshly minted slogan of 'minimum government, maximum governance', the Central as well as the State governments are under pressure to extend their reach to more and more economic, social and personal areas—genetically modified crops, adoption, surrogacy, education (of the young and the old), protection and welfare (of unborn babies as well as the brain-dead), and appear to have proceeded much beyond Adam Smith's conception of a government's functions—"tolerable administration of justice, peace, and supply of public goods"[1].

## From macro to micro governance

It is difficult to take sides on the issue whether governments need to have their finger in every social and economic pie or let citizens be *'Free To Choose'*[2] as Milton Friedman would have it. The debate, however, seems to miss the point. Government is in a way, a public good very much in demand except may be for those who would love to replace it. J.K. Galbraith's remark seems very appropriate: "To a far greater degree than is commonly supposed, functions accrue to the state because as a purely technical matter, there is no alternative to public management."[3] Steve Hilton, who is an avid advocate of a human approach to public policy, has put it in perspective: "Business does not run the world. In the end, government sets the rules by which business—and everyone else—operates."[4] The question, therefore, is not whether, but how to govern. It is suggested that this requires a shift from macro governance, vision documents and grand plans and policies, to micro governance and the small nodes of governance interactions between the people and the 'street level bureaucracy', or what Soman calls the 'last mile.'[5]

## Why the 'Last Mile' matters

Governments need to focus on the 'last mile' for a number of reasons. The 'first mile' in governance—making a policy—is rarely a problem; social and economic policies and regulations are now framed only after extensive consultations and, thanks to the aggressive NGOs, generally reflect broad public consensus and enlightened opinion. Second, most of the government policies and regulations are directed at optimising public welfare; it is rare for a democratic government to deliberately exploit or manipulate its citizens, even though practice may not always be perfect. Most of these policies, however, fail or fall short of their objectives due to the 'intention-implementation' gap. And sometimes the intended beneficiaries and target groups themselves may not access or avail of benefits and services due to ignorance or other reasons.

## Behavioural approach: what it means

Kahneman refers[6] to the distinctive role the two selves or cognitive systems, the intuitive System 1 and the deliberative System 2. Thaler and Sunstein refer[7] to System 1 as an 'automatic system'—'uncontrolled, effortless, associative, fast, unconscious, skilled' and System 2 as a 'reflective system'—'controlled, effortful, deductive, slow, self-aware, and rule-following'. It is generally agreed that it is the intuitive and fast thinking System I, rather than the rational and logical System 2 which plays a major role in making choices, judgements and decisions. Further, our behaviour and actions are affected not only by emotions, as is well known, but also by cognitive heuristics (rules of the thumb or mental short cuts) and biases which underpin System 1. Maria Konnikova has insightfully described the decision making System I as the Watson or credulous system and System 2 as the Sherlock Holmes or logical system.[8]

A number of affective and cognitive heuristics and biases (framing, availability, representativeness, anchoring, risk avoidance for loss but risk appetite for gain, confirmation bias, overconfidence, myopia, status quo bias) have been identified by behavioural scientists. Richard Nisbett has provided an excellent exposition of different heuristics and biases in *Mindware*[9]. What governments need, however, is not a very sophisticated and expert application of these findings but to orient their antennae, while designing policy and institutions, to the working of the human brain, the dominance of System I in judgement, choice and decision making, and to factor in the aspect of behaviour compatibility in the context and situation of a particular policy, regulation or intervention. What governments need is not 'relationship managers' and 'salesman' to promote macro policies but a behaviourally informed rule-design centred on the human subjects, their motives, incentives, behavioural characteristics and biases and how they think and behave. As the Nobel prize-winners Akerlof and Schiller remark, "whenever it (government) designs policy for influencing the actions and behaviour of citizens, it needs to take note of their actual behaviour,"[10] not only their rationality and self interest but also the 'monkey on the shoulder'—"weaknesses, heuristics and biases (informational and psychological)."[11]

## Self interest and the rational actor model

While public policy, rules and practice need to take note of the behaviour of the actors involved in governance interactions, this does not imply negating self interest and the rational actor model. Cialdini, who has authored an influential book on how cheats and manipulators exploit human weakness to defraud customers, clients and the general public, defines self interest thus: "people want to get the most and pay the least for their choices."[12] While listing six traits which, though far removed from the rational actor model, are generally used for persuading or manipulating people—consistency, reciprocation, social proof, authority, liking and scarcity—he remarks: "I choose not to treat material self interest separately; it is a motivational given that deserves acknowledgement but not extensive description."[13] Behavioural economists Gneezy and List observe: "self interest is at the root of human motivation and once we find what people really value, we can devise appropriate triggers and mechanisms needed to change their behaviour."[14] System 1 in fact is an intuitive survival kit underpinned by self interest.

In fact, the rational actor model may be a good enough guide in many areas of governance. *The Birth and Death Registration Act* in India mandates that the family is responsible for reporting the events of birth and death. While families would have some interest in reporting the death of a parent as succession issues may be involved, they may have little motivation to report the death of newborns and infants. Now that we have the health workers—ANMs (Auxiliary Nurse and Midwife) and ASHA (Accredited Social Health Associate) workers—in each village, just shifting the onus of reporting from the uninterested family to these health workers may be enough to help develop a reliable base of primary data on infant mortality for which we have to rely on surveys at present. The book provides a number of similar examples where policies, rules and institutions would do well to appeal directly to self interest; human beings may not be always rational but they are not therefore necessarily and 'predictably irrational.'[15]

## Rules and institutions: the 'choice architects' of behaviour

One distinctive feature of public governance is that the context may itself be structured and 'framed' by *formal* and *codified* statutes, rules and institutions, unlike economic and social exchanges which are shaped primarily by *informal* and *customary* institutions and norms. Douglass North defined[16] institutions as rules of the game, though he was more concerned with macro social and economic institutions such as property rights. These rules of the game define and shape how the game is played. Take the game of soccer or football. Rules defining the dimensions of the play ground are relevant in deciding what ability to look for in players. If the playground were to be one mile long, coaches would probably look for marathon runners rather than sprinters to play as forwards. Such decisions are made before the game begins. On the other hand, rules about what constitutes a foul or an off-side determine how the game is played. A proper design of the institutions or operational rules of the game is therefore a *sine qua non* for influencing the responses and behaviour of various actors and for bridging the 'intention-implementation gap'. These rules are in fact the 'choice architects' which influence the responses and behaviour of the public, clients and customers, unlike the business world where the role of choice architects is performed mostly by human agents—sales and marketing staff. Departmental stores design the display of the goods to lure customers to buy high priced goods; cheaper substitutes, which may be good enough, are pushed to the back shelves or inconspicuous corners. In public governance, it is the agency of rules rather than the human agents which creates the structure of external influences, 'choice architecture'[17] or 'social environment' for any policy or intervention and that's why the rules need a behaviourally informed design.

## Designing rules for humans

Don Norman has pointed out that the design of rules and institutions needs as much attention as physical objects: "Services, lectures, rules and procedures, and the organisational structures of businesses and governments do not have physical mechanisms, but their rules of operation have to be designed, sometimes informally, sometimes precisely recorded and specified."[18] He indicates three focus areas for a 'human centred design'—industrial design, interactive design and experience design; while the industrial designers focus on form and material, interactive designers emphasize understandability and usability, and experience designers the emotional impact. As indicated above, the government rules, institutions and regulations require a 'human centred design' even more than physical objects. Moreover, policy and rules makers need to focus not so much on form (bureaucratic check lists, forms, procedures and so on) or experience (police should offer a chair to the accused who may be beaten black and blue later) as they tend to do, but on an interactive design of the governance rules and institutions and the ease and comfort with which they are understood and used by the people involved in governance interactions.

## Mandates, nudges and default rules

Rules have traditionally been designed around the traditional carrots and sticks (mostly the latter in India) and a human-centred design is very much needed to reinforce the dated governance armoury and toolkit. The institutions of default options and mild 'nudges' are especially appropriate for replacing and/or reinforcing regulatory bans and mandates. Default rules facilitate choice by providing default options for those who may find it difficult to make a choice and can be, as Sunstein remarks,[19] even more effective sometimes than material incentives. I had given an example of the power of a default rule in *Governance Unbound*.[20] The size of food plates and portions of servings can be very powerful defaults in tackling the problem of obesity.[21] Moreover, while carrots are known to be more effective than sticks generally, in some contexts, mandates and statutory bans may be necessary. Unfortunately, as in the case of health promotion, public policy seems to be driven mostly by ideology: "most of the policy efforts have predominantly targeted System 2 and disregarded System I."[22]

## Limitations, challenges and opportunities

What is being proposed is not a miracle cure. Genetics provide an analogy. We know now that there are no specific genes for criminality or for most of the genetic diseases and we no longer expect genetic editing of a particular gene or a strand of the DNA to work wonders. Proponents of the behavioural approach have themselves been very modest in making such claims. David Halpern has pointed out[23] various risks and limitations. And not everybody behaves and responds in the same fashion. Even a very innovative 'nudge' may leave some 'econs' unaffected. In the case of Soloman Asch experiments of the 1950s, a substantial minority (over 25%) did not succumb to majority pressure. In fact that is precisely the plus point of a behavioural approach; it is ideally equipped to address the elements both of universality and diversity of *Homo sapiens*.

Behavioural economics and experimental psychology have shown that sensitivity to and awareness of the behavioural dimensions of public policy can bring about a sea change not only in terms of efficiency and cost but also the policy outcomes. It is, however, difficult to devise a neat quantitative model to prove its relevance for public governance. It is rare to find universal endorsement of even path-breaking research findings as there is little academic premium in confirmatory research. Further, a particular situation may involve multiple behavioural factors and cognitive and emotional biases; anticipating what will work in a particular situation is not easy. David Halpern gives the example of how the 'scared straight' programme, getting teenagers to visit prisons to see for themselves the miserable life in prisons and thus 'nudge' them against leading a life of crime, may have the opposite effect, of imprinting criminal behaviour as a norm. Moreover, the laboratory and field experiments need to be scaled up for application in real life situations and this requires experience, knowledge as well as a lot of tenacity, as David Halpern's experience of working for the UK government shows.[24] All said and done, however, this is the best bet we have got for improving governance outcomes.

## Do we need the RCTs?

Randomized Controlled Trials (RCTs) can be helpful and may be necessary for scaling up such interventions. It is, however, difficult for a government to conduct such experiments; probably it is difficult even to accept and adopt the findings of the RCTs, as the example given in Chapter 12 shows. In any case, we don't need to reinvent the wheel and probably know enough even now, thanks to academic and field research and case studies. In a Chapter titled *What Works*[25], Halpern has provided graphics indicating the cost benefit of popular interventions and strategies in education and health. In India, the pupil-teacher ratio still dominates the discourse on reform, even though it is one of the least cost effective options. It has been known[26] for a long time that de-worming programmes can greatly help school children in areas where open defecation is common but India has introduced this as a major plank of its health policy only in 2015. Similar is the case with policy directed at malnutrition of children; supply of fortified foods can be an effective intervention. We can surely make use of this default option and offer fortified foods in the mid day meals programme in schools; parents can opt out if they so desire.

## Addressing behavioural governance failure

As I hope to demonstrate, we need to improve the design of rules and regulations rather than blame corrupt or inefficient agents, ineffective structures and inadequate resources for governance failure. What Sunstein calls 'behavioural market failure'[27] is probably more appropriately described, in the case of public governance, as behavioural governance failure which is many a time occasioned by a neglect of how human beings are likely to behave in specific contexts and situations, and needs to be addressed by a behaviourally informed and 'human centred design' of the government policies, rules and regulations. Policy makers require what Richard Nisbett calls "pragmatic reasoning schemas"[28] or rule systems. These 'schemas' include basics like cost benefit analysis and opportunity cost (economics), regression to be mean (statistics), Occam's razor (logic), as also affective and cognitive heuristics and biases (behavioural sciences); in fact it seems to me that what he is suggesting are simply templates and frameworks based on plain common sense, with a little more weight to the last dimension - of behaviour. As mentioned earlier, while the macro policy may be very well structured, the operational rules or rules of the game tend to be designed in a somewhat cavalier manner by the aggressive but automatic System 1 of those who design the rules. For example, even though objectives of the two laws—one for the donation of organs and the other for granting a licence for a factory - could not be more different, their procedures, checklists, forms and rules are cooked in the same pot, as two of the chapters will demonstrate. Above all, therefore, governments need to give a lot of attention to the design of these rules, which are, in Kaushik Basu's words[29], the plumbing and the nuts and bolts of public policy.

## Endnotes

1 Smith, Adam, 1776/1978, *The Wealth of Nations,* pp. 240-5, Penguin Books, UK.
2 Friedman, Milton and Friedman, Rose, 1980/1990, *Free to Choose,* Harvest Books/Harcourt.
3 (quoted in) Cassidy, John, 2009, *How Markets Fail,* Allen Lane, Penguin Group.
4 Hilton, Steve, 2015, *More Human: Designing A World Where People Come First,* WH Allen, UK.
5 Soman, Dilip, 2015, *The Last Mile, Creating Social and Economic Value from Behavioural Insights,* University of Toronto.
6 Kahneman, Daniel, 2011, *Thinking Fast & Slow,* Farrar, Straus & Giroux, New York.
7 Thaler, Richard H. and Sunstein, Cass R., 2008, *Nudge: Improving Decisions About Health, Wealth, and Happiness,* Yale University Press, New Haven.
8 Konnikova, Maria, 2013, *Mastermind: How To Think Like Sherlock Holmes,* Viking Penguin, New York/Cannongate Books, Edinburgh.
9 Nisbett, Richard E., 2015, *Mindware: Tools for Smart Thinking,* Allen Lane, P. 117.
10 Akerlof, A. and Schiller, Robert J., 2015, *Phishing for Phools: The Economics of Manipulation and Deception,* Princeton University Press.
11 Akerlof et al, Ibid.
12 Cialdini, Robert B., 2009, *Influence: The Psychology of Persuasion,* Harper Collins ebook.
13 Cialdini, 2009, Ibid.
14 Gneezy, Uri and List, John, 2013, *The Why Axis: Hidden Motives and the Undiscovered Economics of Everyday Life,* Penguin Random House, UK.
15 Ariely, Dan, 2010, *Predictably Irrational,* Harper Collins, UK.
16 North, Douglass, 1990/2007, *Institutions, Institutional Change and Economic Performance,* Cambridge University Press.
17 Thaler and Sunstein, 2008, Ibid.

18 Norman, Don, 1988/2013, *The Design of Everyday Things*, Basic Books, New York.

19 Sunstein, Cass R., 2015, *Choosing Not To Choose: Understanding the Value of Choice*, Oxford University Press e-book.

20 Example of a Default Rule in Action in a Power Utility: Power supply to the agriculture sector was not free, but the State of Punjab had a flat rate (Rs. X per HP—Horse Power - of the tubewell motor). The records showed an overwhelming number of motors to be of 3 HP, whereas the pressure of the water-guzzling paddy crop had led to most of the motors having been actually upgraded to 5 HP by the farmers; the official procedure for upgrading of the motors was not only expensive but also tortuous. The question for the utility was: 'how to identify such cases and levy higher charges'? Random checks, penalties, and exhortations were not helpful. The utility finally adopted, after trial and error, a new strategy: instructions were issued that all motors would be billed at 5 HP, unless any farmer declared to the utility that he/she had a 3 HP motor, which claim could be verified and power supply disconnected in the case of false claims. The farmers in Punjab are a strong lobby and, as such, managed through political pressures to have the period provided for exercising the option extended twice. But, ultimately they acquiesced in the default option; their System I was too strong"!

21 Alemanno, A., *A Behavioural Approach to Health Promotion: Informing Global NCD Agenda with Behavioural Insights (www.albertoalemanno. ed)*.

22 Alemanno, Ibid.

23 Halpern, David, 2015, *Inside the Nudge Unit: How Small Changes Can Make a Big Difference*, W.H. Allen.

24 Halpern, 2015, Ibid.

25 Ibid.

26 Banerjee, Abhijit and Duflo, Esther, 2011, *Poor Economics: Rethinking Poverty and the Ways to End It*, Random House India.

27 Sunstein, Cass R., 2013, *Simpler: The Future of Government*, Simon and Schuster ebook.

28 Nisbett, 2015, Ibid.

29 Basu, Kaushik, 2016, *An Economist in the Real World: The Art of Policymaking in India*, Penguin/Viking.

# 1

# Donation of Organs
## Framework of a Human Policy

The market for the purchase and sale of organs including blood was almost universal till about seventy years back. Titmuss's work[1] on voluntary donation of blood was the game-changer which shifted the paradigm from trading to donation of organs. Commercial transactions, however, continue, as has been graphically documented by Scott Carney[2]. Despite the dissenting voices of some economists who propagate market solutions, most people find the concept of marketization to be morally repugnant. The dominant social norm is that donations should be voluntary—whether blood or kidneys or whatever. Iran is one of the few exceptions and that also only for kidneys. The problem of a huge gap between demand and supply, however, continues, especially in countries like India, where even the basic physical, regulatory and technical infrastructure is still at a nascent stage. Behavioural economists have suggested some soft and moderate interventions to encourage people to volunteer. One is that of 'presumed consent'; a person is presumed to have given consent to be a donor, unless he/she chooses to opt out; consent is the 'default option'. Spain, Austria and some other countries which have adopted these practices are doing much better. Richard Thaler, the co-author of the famous book *Nudge* has advocated this approach.

The policy in India appears to be driven almost entirely by ideology and a moralistic frame, and such behavioural nudges and incentives are rarely considered seriously by the framers of laws and regulations. The Transplantation of Human Organs and Tissues Act 1994 proclaims the two main objectives to be prevention of trading in organs and promotion of donations. As will be seen, however, most of the operational rules, procedures and processes of donation and harvesting of organs reflect a bias towards the first objective of preventing trafficking in human organs rather than promotion of voluntary donations. All that the law has succeeded in doing, therefore, is to discourage donation of organs, whether by live donors, the relatives and friends of the recipients, or even anonymous public spirited donors. One of the two objectives of the statute has thus been defeated by the very rules meant to achieve them.

## Donations by relatives and friends

Multiple gatekeepers have been provided under the rules to prevent misuse in the case of the relatives and friends who volunteer to donate their organs for specific recipients. The rules have been framed primarily to prevent exploitation of the poor who may be tempted by monetary incentives to donate their organs, while posing as relatives, well-wishers and friends. The rules (Form 1c of the Rules) require even the vocation and income of the donor to be stated and sworn under oath by the donor! Attestation by a notary is also mandatory. The law requires detailed documentation about identity, relationship and willingness to donate, which is scrutinised by the authorisation committee responsible for ensuring that the donation is not commercial and does not involve any middleman.

While the authorisation committees are expected to filter such cases and sift the wheat from the chaff, all they have to go by is documentation. Though the committee's decisions, taken in good faith, are protected, it may have neither the time nor the inclination nor even the capacity to indulge in time consuming enquiries. Such decisions moreover have a constraint; they are urgent and leave little time for field visits and detailed enquiries. *The end result is that even well meaning and dedicated officials who are members of these committees may end up mostly with the only rational and safe choice—rejection of unrelated donors who claim bonds of friendship or affection with the recipient, lest they be accused of wrong doing; rejection becomes the default choice.*

## Rules for public donors

The tortuous procedures in the case of unrelated donors could possibly be justified the ground that such precautions are necessary to prevent trafficking of organs. Unfortunately the rules for public donors pledging donation of the organs after death are no different. Form 5 of the rules provides that even a public donor who donates his/her organs after death *must* have a near relative as one of the two witnesses, even though the donation is not meant for any particular recipient. The donation has also to be made "unequivocally". In fact the design of the rules and forms sends strong but perverse signals that donation may not be a very prestigious act. In any case, the rules do not make it easy to make a donation, not to speak of providing incentives, which may be necessary even for charities, as has been shown by Uri Gneezy and John List[3]. The rules also offend one's sense of dignity and autonomy. Why do I need a near relative to witness the authorization even when I am not nominating any recipient as the live donors do? No wonder most of the donations in India are from relatives and friends who, for reasons of affection and love, may be motivated enough to go through and endure the tortuous and difficult processes. Acts of altruistic donation are therefore rare, a consequence mostly of the very rules meant to promote donations.

## Harvesting of organs

Rules for the medical officers who have to authorize harvesting of donated organs posthumously are no better. This may be the reason that in India only a negligible share of transplantation of organs is contributed by cadaver organs. Section 1A of the Act requires the Registered Medical Practitioner working in a hospital to:

   (i) ascertain from the patient admitted to the ICU (or his near relative) whether he/she is a donor;

   (ii) o make the patient/relative aware about the options available;

   (iii) in cases where no authorisation is available and no objection is expressed, organs of persons after death may be authorised for removal *unless "he has reason to believe that no near relative of the deceased person has objection to such use"*.

Similarly as per Section 5, in the case of unclaimed bodies in hospitals, transplantation can be authorised if any near relative has not claimed the body within 48 hours of the time of death *provided that "no authority should be given if the person empowered to give such authority has reason to believe that any near relative of the deceased person is likely to claim the dead body even though such near relative has not come forward to claim the body of the deceased person within the time specified"*.

In the first place, the very first steps of checking and creating awareness [(i) and (ii) above] and so on are somewhat vague and not likely to be complied with; the doctors in the ICUs are always under tremendous work pressure. The duty rosters keep changing, thus diffusing the responsibility of individual doctors. In practice, donations are mostly secured through the efforts of the NGO volunteers who visit the ICUs and the wards. Second, there is little incentive for the doctors to fulfil these formalities; a doctor is unlikely to risk his/her career as a relative can always appear later. Moreover, most of the organs become unfit for use after 48 hours. *And what's more, the onus remains on the doctor to be satisfied that no relatives will appear later.* The rules are a sure recipe, not for promoting donations of organs, but for the doctors to adopt the safe course of doing nothing which in this case means not authorising harvesting; denying permission for harvesting is therefore very likely to be the default choice.

The consequence of these rules is prevalence of underground trade and surreptitious removal of organs, especially eyes (which are relatively easy to retrieve), of the unclaimed bodies, with or without collusion. *The whole institutional structure of authorization committees, procedure for matching donations and harvesting of cadaver organs is designed to discourage rather than promote donations.* The *'Red Market'*[4] continues to flourish.

## Presumed consent and mandated choice

The question is, can some imaginative 'nudges' help? 'Thaler et al.'[5] devote a chapter to the relevance of 'nudges' for increasing organ donations: moving from 'explicit consent' to 'presumed consent' or if this is socially and politically not feasible, to 'mandated choice'. The latter implies that every person is required to tick one of the two boxes 'yes, willing to donate' or 'no, unwilling to donate'. The example of a dramatic nudge, mentioned in *Nudge*, is the Illinois First Person Consent Registry law, which declares the choice of the First Person (donor) to be absolute; no further consent is required from the donor's family. A change in law on the lines of the Illinois one, coupled with 'mandated choice' for all the holders of driving licences, would probably work wonders in India.

## Optimising donations: 'Timing'

In the case of donation of organs, the factor of timing as mentioned[6] by Halpern is material especially in India, where the law provides a conscious 'opt in' choice, without any default rule. The appropriate time for pledging the donation appears to be when a driving licence is issued. Most of the adults need a licence, one time or the other, and one can make a carefully considered decision at that time without being buffeted by contrary bits of advice from friends and relatives at a time of emotional and cognitive vulnerability; it is difficult for a person to be cool and rational as he/she approaches the moment of death. One may become unduly religious, get concerned about after-life, more so if the family/friends who may be opposed to donation are standing by; or more likely, he/she may not decide; *doing nothing* and a status quo bias is an attractive option in such situations.

Linking the act of donation to issue of a driving licence will ensure the genuineness and authenticity of the donation as well as the donor. Moreover, we need a massive base of donors—say 10,000 donors for one transplant recipient keeping in view the death rate and the demand and this system of donation is possibly the best logistic for optimising the number of public donors. Donation will be an authentic act as the pledge is far away in time from the occasion when the donation may be invoked. The only issue for the government to decide is whether to provide an 'opt in' option—a person must sign the declaration to be a donor or an 'opt out' option (in that case 'presumed consent' is the default).

## Designing a default list of organs

Apart from policy design, the design of operational rules also matters in shaping responses. One instance is the format used at present for making donations which has not been carefully designed. The donation form requires a donor to list each organ separately and even a list of organs is not provided (Form 5).This may result is most of the people simply mentioning the organ which is easily recalled; System 1 is in action in such matters of choice. The formats of the donation pledges need to be redesigned to encourage a donor to donate more than one organ. Probably *a default bouquet or list of organs* to be donated could be provided, rather than leaving it to donors to have to choose and check boxes for a long list. For example, the main internal organs (liver, heart, kidneys, lungs,) could be the default list. The reason is that donation of the whole body and the external organs (skin, eyes) may not be very popular for aesthetic and religious reasons; some of us may not like their dead body to be disfigured. A default option will therefore help optimize the number of organs donated by each individual even though the numbers of donors remain the same. And an entry in the driving licence should be considered a conclusive proof of donation, not requiring relatives' clearance or endorsement for harvesting; relatives will accept the choice of the deceased once the ambiguity in law about the role and voice of relatives is removed.

Autonomy of the donor is even more necessary in the case of a terminally ill person. It is unlikely that most of the families would push for a decision to donate and even one 'no' may be enough for an effective veto. And families may also be more bothered about the hassle of removing the organ donated and the consequent disruption in the ablution and cremation rituals. Democratic societies value the freedom of choice of individuals but surprisingly the Act allows the family to have a say by mandating a near relation to be a witness. *The choice of the donor in the presence of any witness, not necessarily a family member, needs to be treated as absolute except in the case of live donors and of course the brain-dead.*

## Algorithms for matching donors and recipients

Another major problem is that of matching donors and recipients and genetic matching and compatibility between the recipient and the donor. Matching requirements differ depending on the organs and tissues involved. As Davis points out[7], most of the organ transplants need matching between the recipient and the potential donor across a number of compatibility genes; the status of immune reactivity against the donor cells also needs to be checked. The quality of matching is also important; it can affect the life of the graft. Supply of organs suitable for transplants, therefore, is likely to remain limited. A willing relative or friend, even though able to get through rigorous vetting procedures, may not necessarily be suitable as a donor due to these matching requirements. Simplistic solutions which depend on volunteerism and have worked, though in a limited way, in the case of blood donation, may not therefore be adequate for skin grafts, kidney, heart, bone marrow and other organ transplants. Some practical solutions to improve the rate of transplantation of kidneys by matching pairs of incompatible patient-donor units have been suggested[8] by Alvin Roth and others and these have led to a substantial improvement in the rate of transplantation in some of the US states. Such simple measures, supported by appropriate rules, may be successful even without having to compromise with the high ethical principles which form the basis of the present set of laws and regulations. Regulations in India already provide for a barter or exchange between two needy families where the profile of family 'A' donor matches the profile of the recipient in family 'B' and vice versa but matching algorithms can cover three, four or even more pairs as Alvin Roth shows[9] and can thus be much more socially productive.

Iran has solved the problem of shortage of donors for kidneys by having a state aided incentive cum compensation programme for the unrelated donors who may be paid $1,200-2,000 by the government and the charitable institutions, apart from free health insurance offered by the government to the donor. As indicated, however, the government can bring about a sea change even without changing the basic laws simply by tweaking the operational rules and even without having to adopt the Iranian module:

(i) All driving licences to carry information on the status of the licencee as a donor; further authentication or endorsement of relatives should not be necessary for harvesting organs in such cases.

(ii) Driving licence holders to be given a choice to opt out as has been done in the UK; the default rule will be 'presumed consent' if one does not opt out. If that is not feasible, we need to provide at least '*mandated choice*' —each applicant *must choose* whether to be a donor or otherwise.

(iii) Designing a default list of organs to be donated. This will increase the number of organs donated per donor.

(iv) In the case of patients who are admitted in a hospital at least 24 hours before their death, the MOs to be unequivocally authorised to allow harvesting of cadaver organs, in case no relative claims the body within a specific time period, without any 'ifs' and 'buts' of the present rules.

# Endnotes

1 Titmuss, Richard M., 1970, *The Gift Relationship: From Human Blood to Social Policy*, in (ed) Ann Oakley and John Ashton, The New Press 1997.

2 Carney, Scott, 2011, *The Red Market: On the Trail of the World's Organ Brokers, Bone Thieves, Blood Farmers and Child Traffickers*, William Morrow/Harper Collins ebook.

3 Gneezy, Uri and List, John, 2013, *The Why Axis: Hidden Motives and the Undiscovered Economics of Everyday Life*, Penguin Random House, UK.

4 Carney, 2011, Ibid.

5 Thaler, et al, 2008, Ibid.

6 Halpern, David, 2015, *Inside the Nudge Unit: How Small Changes Can Make a Big Difference*, W.H. Allen.

7 Davis, Daniel M., 2013, *The Compatibility Gene*, Allen Lane/Penguin Books.

8 Roth, Alvin E., Sonmez, Tayfun, Unver, M. Utku, 2004, Kidney Exchange, *The Quarterly Journal and Economics*, May 2004.

9 Roth, Alvin E., 2015, *Who Gets What And Why: The Hidden World of Matchmaking and Market Design*, William Collins/Harper Collins, Indian Edition.

# 2

# Female Foeticide
## Even Inhuman Acts need Human Rules*

The Pre-Conception and Pre-natal Diagnostic Techniques (PCPNDT) Act passed in the year 1994 and amended in 2003 is the main policy instrument in India for redressing adverse sex ratio. The law is now (after the 2003 amendment) much more stringent but nowhere near being the game changer it was hoped to be. Demographic trends, as reflected in the Sample Registration System (SRS) and the census figures, are somewhat mixed in respect of different states and economic, social and population groups but the broad picture continues to cause serious concern. Recent data based on the CRS (Central Registration System) and the SRS (Sample Registration System) does not provide much cause for optimism; provisional data for Punjab and Chandigarh UT shows that the situation may be getting worse.

While the CSR (Child Sex Ratio) and OSR (Overall Sex Ratio) do matter, there is a need to focus on the BSR (Sex Ratio at Birth). The programmes of mass vaccination like *Indradhanush* and maternal and child care and health are likely to help eliminate the imbalance in the CSR and the OSR over the next few years. The rate of improvement in

---

* Based on a monograph: Gupta, R.N., 2015, *Female Foeticide: Designing A Public Policy For Humans,* Institute for Development and Communication, Chandigarh.

infant and child mortality during the last few years has been broadly moving at par for males and females. Second, the BSR is the main contributor to gender imbalance—over 5% in India and as high as 8% in some of the states. Third, in the case of sex ratio at birth, we need to factor in the countervailing family incentives, male child preference and so on, which result in a large number of *conscious* acts of female foeticide. We need to focus, therefore, in the words of Dreze and Sen[1], on "prenatal rather than post natal discrimination".

### Sex Ratio in India

|        | 1961 | 1971 | 1981 | 1991 | 2001 | 2011 |
|--------|------|------|------|------|------|------|
| CSR    | 976  | 964  | 962  | 945  | 927  | 918  |
| OSR    | 941  | 930  | 934  | 926  | 933  | 943  |
| BSR    | 994  | 989  | 967  | 939  | 915  | 910  |

The table shows the apparently negligible impact of the stringent law, the PCPNDT Act. As the BSR figures from 1981 to 2001 indicate, sex ratio has worsened over the period of around twenty years the law has been in operation. It is also difficult to argue that the position could have been much worse in the absence of the PNDT Act.

## Institutions and clinical practices

A number of contextual factors shift the odds against the present policy. The data available with the government institutions and the NFHS (National Family Health Survey) and discussions with professional service-providers and the enforcement agencies, appear to indicate that registered clinics may be responsible only for a fraction (10% to 30%) of the scans carried out for the purpose of disclosure of sex of the foetus. The present focus on enforcement directed at the registered scanning centres and approved MTP (Medical Termination of Pregnancy) clinics, therefore, appears misplaced. In any case, it is well known that female foetuses are mostly aborted outside the institutions approved for this purpose. Moreover, the deterrent effect of the tough punishments provided under the law is diluted by various factors. Obtaining a conviction is difficult as the act of disclosure of sex does not leave any evidence, document or 'digiprint'. There is little scope for the use of decoys and whistleblowers who can provide reliable evidence for conviction; such acts are private and there may not be much incentive for a third party to blow the whistle. Another major constraint is that the enforcement staff lacks information. It is no wonder, therefore, that only about 25% of the total prosecutions relate to substantive offences; the rest are about technical violations.

There is another relevant factor—moral ambiguity created by the MTP Act. The basic premise of the Medical Termination of Pregnancy Act (MTP) is the freedom of choice of the involved women, whereas the PCPNDT Act seeks to restrict such choices. This ambivalence is likely to pull human agents in different directions. The MTP Act may in fact provide some moral support for a rationalisation of the (illegal) acts of abortion of female foetuses. Even the enforcement officials may sometimes hesitate in choosing between the competing objectives of family planning (the MTP Act) and gender balance (PNDT Act). Moreover, the present law (MTP) Act is liberal and a foetus can be aborted, inter alia, on the ground of failure of contraceptive devices; the woman reporting for abortion may have knowledge about sex of the foetus but the doctor has no way to find out or deny her the right to have the abortion.

## Social cost of regulations

We also need to consider the substantial social cost imposed by these regulations; the cost is in terms of the tremendous material and psychological costs borne by the agencies and actors on the demand side (pain, anxiety, guilt suffered by the involved women and sometimes family discord) as well as the supply side clinics (cost of filling up and maintenance of forms and returns which are rarely analysed, coping with inspections). A pragmatic regulatory design should take note of these social costs.

## Free-rider problem

One additional problem in the case of public goods like gender balance is free riding; one can benefit from a healthy sex ratio while simultaneously personally benefitting (may be not really but the belief is what matters) from sex selective practices. Public affirmations, resolutions and so on may not therefore affect personal behaviour.

## A behavioural perspective

The interventions and changes usually advocated such as *increasing the scale of punishment to provide deterrence, tracking of pregnant women, remote sensors for recording scanning activity and more and more of inspections, meetings and 'raids'*, which are mostly whimsical and ad hoc, mainly due to the problem of information about malpractices, may not be of much help. Conventional wisdom leads to more and more of the same ineffective medicine and a social cost benefit analysis will not have much to show on the credit side, except for tons of paper and gigabytes of digital data. A different paradigm is needed for the government to achieve the desired outcome of a healthy sex ratio at birth and a behavioural perspective may provide at least a partial solution.

A behavioural or behaviourally informed approach simply means that we should factor in the motives, incentives and behaviour of the concerned actors and agents while designing rules, schemes and regulations. This also means, as mentioned in *Introduction,* that we need to design regulations directed not only at the rationality of the actors but also their motives, incentives and the cognitive limitations and biases.

## Cultural, social and emotional factors

Most of the regions and population groups are known to have a preference for male children. This is no doubt due to a number of cultural and social factors which were responsible for the practice of female infanticide which appears to have been quite common till the 1st half of the 20th century. Female infanticide is probably rare now, as relatively clean options for aborting foetuses have become available and it is no longer a social norm. On the other hand, while cultural and social factors may contribute to female foeticide, we also need to consider the countervailing emotional factor of the parent's affection for own progeny, whether a child or just a foetus or embryo and the bond which even a foetus forms quickly not only with the mother but also with other family members and siblings. To some extent, even in the case of sex selective abortions, one needs to factor in this aspect of loss and pain suffered by the family/mother in the process of losing the foetus. Michael Sherman has captured this aspect in a chapter: *A Moral Science of Women's Rights* of his book[2], *The Moral Arc.* He quotes Edward Tylor's anthropological observation made in the 19th century: "Infanticide arises from hardness of life rather than hardness of heart". As Sherman remarks "Normal people do not kill their children for no reason" and like all human behaviour "infanticide has non-trivial causes". *The decision to abort a male or a female foetus is a painful one and instead of devising harsh punishments for mothers and couples, one may need to consider what (in their view) may be the potential benefits gained or losses avoided, forcing them to take the painful decision of aborting a female foetus.* It is somewhat difficult for governments to influence socio-cultural factors but they *need to take note at least of economic motivations which are evidently strong enough to overcome and suppress the bonds of affection and compel a family to harm the female foetus and about which governments may be able to something.*

## Motivation and incentives of the demand side actors

The main economic incentives which drive families to female foeticide would appear to be:

(a) that a son will look after parents in old age, unlike a daughter who after marriage by convention leaves the home of parents;

(b) dowry; it can be assumed to be a minimum of Rs. 1-2 lac (at today's prices) for the lower income groups and Rs. 5-10 lacs for the middle class families, and a policy is needed to aggressively counter these drivers of family behaviour.

## Motivation and incentives of suppliers of services

Supply side incentives do not appear strong enough for the registered clinics to undertake illegal practices; risks for professionals are high compared to returns. The result is a grey market run by quacks and unqualified persons for whom this may be the primary, if not the only, source of earning money. Most of the regulatory pressure is however on the registered clinics and translates into filling forms and maintaining records and registers.

## Mistimed and insufficient incentives

Most of the schemes such as *Balri Rakshak Yojna* (Girl Protection Scheme), designed for promoting girl-child preference, are unlikely to have much impact. They seek to provide modest and graded assistance annually for the girl child with a modest sum (of around Rs. 1 lac) expected to accumulate at maturity. Such schemes seem to ignore the cognitive bias of hyperbolic discounting (also known as temporal inconsistency or time preference); future benefits are heavily discounted as compared to present costs. The amount of Rs. 1 lac which may be available to the girl after 20 years, after discounting by a human, male or female, would be equal only to Rs. 5000 or so in hand today. This can hardly be considered sufficient enough to offset the perceived cost of a female child. We know of the Stanford University marsh-mellow studies on delayed gratification among children. In the case of six year olds in America, one study[3] found time preference to be 150% per month, this was the extra reward required to delay instant gratification. Adults may not display such extreme preferences for immediate gratification but the fact is that incentives and gains available in the remote future appear disproportionately small compared to the looming present costs. Such incentives need to be provided *at the time* the choice, whether or not to abort the female foetus, is made by the mother or family. And incentives need to match the perceived costs; there is little point in providing token incentives as governments seem to be doing at present.

Moreover, if the government considers cultural and social factors to be primarily responsible for the neglect of female children, the money would only give rise to a 'moral hazard'—families can pocket the money but still neglect the girl-child, infant or adolescent!

Similarly the well intentioned scheme for giving awards to panchayats who show the best sex ratios, does not appear to be well considered. The law of small numbers is applicable in cases involving small demographic units. It may be just by chance that a panchayat happens to have a high sex ratio in any particular year; it may be just the reverse next year. It is unlikely that such schemes will have any impact, as even the Panchayats receiving the award won't know what they have done to deserve it!

## Female foeticide policy: behavioural governance failure

Consensus among the academics, critics or supporters, and the administrators is that neither the regulatory apparatus for enforcement nor the programs for awareness and capacity building have been very effective in curbing female foeticide. Solutions, suggestions and prescriptions made in various reports, workshops and evaluations, which are based on what J.K. Galbraith called conventional wisdom appear to have been ineffective. As indicated, promotional incentives such as prize money for Panchayats, education and dowry money for daughters and so on do not appear to be effective or even efficient. The same is the case with negative incentives—penal consequences for mothers/ families and the clinicians. Moreover, one must not forget that harsh punishments may encourage gaming of the rules through corruption and collusion. Creating awareness about the morality and legality of foeticide may also not be very helpful in curbing the practice. It is well established that awareness may affect attitudes but rarely does it affect behaviour, at least not in the short term[4]. So far as the supply side is concerned, as in the case of collusive acts of corruption, we would rarely get evidence which is adequate for prosecution, let alone conviction. It would be no exaggeration to say that the Act is a typical instance of what I have described as behavioural governance failure in *Introduction*.

## Nudging through 'Naming and Shaming'

It may be possible to nudge the families and couples towards socially desirable behaviour though a 'naming and shaming' strategy. This can be done by mandating ultrasound investigation for all pregnant women, recording sex of the foetus and publicising the names of women who abort the female foetus. If mandatory disclosure of sex of the foetus is not feasible or acceptable, governments could at least provide inexpensive and free screening for those who want it and decriminalise sex selective practices, while simultaneously publishing the data for the purpose of 'naming and shaming' or even for reverse motivation of the families concerned. These proposals are advocated by the pro-choice liberals but may not be acceptable or may be considered too risky; a Union Minister made a similar suggestion but it had to be hastily withdrawn following a barrage of protests.

## Proposals for a human policy

While therefore we may have to continue with the present misdirected and ineffective carrots and sticks, some inexpensive measures can help as indicated below.

(a) **Mothers as whistleblowers:** The best bet, as in the case of corruption appears to be the 'invisible foot' strategy,[5] encouraging whistle blowers, in this case the women involved, by providing immunity and even incentives to them, to provide evidence against the clinics which provide illegal services. The strategy is the obverse of the 'invisible hand'; it may effectively reduce illegal collusions by creating distrust among the parties—the doctor and the pregnant woman. The clinics, registered or not, doing illegal scans and sex selective abortions may hastily review their incentives if the woman concerned is empowered to be the whistleblower.

(b) **Proportionality in punishment for minor violations:** Current regulations, which provide for the same punishment, irrespective of the gravity of an offence— technical or substantive—violate the principle of proportionally (see also Chapter 6); they shift attention from outcomes to monitoring of routine activities, outputs and targets of inspection etc., which may have little bearing on the outcomes. As a radiologist told me, doctors are now devoting much more attention and time to records and forms rather than investigation and have practically become clerks. The enforcers as well as the suppliers of services get focussed only on the peripheral and administrative aspects of regulations—maintaining proper registers and forms. *Such regulations in fact not only dilute the authority of and respect for this law, but also for the rule of law in general.*

(c) **A Lottery for pregnant women:** Considering that (a) the threat of punishment and similar disincentives are not likely to work; (b) it is not possible to provide immediate and sufficient incentives to mothers (say Rs.5 lac at the birth of the girl child), we need to devise solutions which don't cost much money but may still provide adequate incentives. *A well designed lottery can be an effective incentive for pregnant women.*

Eligibility should of course be limited to pregnant women who give birth to a girl-child.

## Rationale of the lottery scheme

(i) The proposal is based on a common cognitive failing of humans: lotteries are popular despite negligible odds of winning, as humans overestimate low probabilities.

(ii) Huge resources are not needed for the lottery prizes; *only the winner would get the prize but all the aspirants would have to take steps to retain the female foetus!* Buying or owning a ticket would create a *psychological commitment* not to abort the female foetus.

(iii) *The scheme of a lottery for expecting mothers can provide an immediate and sufficient incentive to a large number of mothers whose psycho-social preferences for male progeny may be marginal.*

Some issues which affect incentives—how to ensure maximum enrolment of pregnant women through voluntary choice, whether to price the ticket, the PR back up for visibility and salience– will of course need to be addressed carefully. The scheme is likely to work because it only requires women to do nothing, the normal human tendency and a 'status quo bias'.

## Incidental benefit—raising the happiness index

The scheme may also serve another social purpose - raising the level of happiness in the society by reducing feelings of guilt and suffering of the family/woman involved as mentioned earlier. In fact, considering the modest sums involved, this ancillary benefit may by itself justify having such a scheme.

## Conclusion

The proposals summarised below may therefore be helpful in addressing this issue:

(a) 'set a thief to catch a thief', the 'invisible foot' strategy for deterring the clinics and other suppliers of illegal services; the suggestion is on the lines of similar changes envisaged in the Prevention of Corruption Act but may be more effective in this case.

(b) Repeal or revoke the provision of incarceration for technical and record keeping violations by the doctors/clinics.

(c) Provide attractive carrots—A lottery scheme for pregnant women with prizes going only to those who give birth to a girl-child; this will not need much resources but would incentivise pregnant women to make socially desirable choices.

The BSR which is based on a one-time choice and decision of the mothers and households concerned is, and can be, influenced by behaviourally informed and properly designed interventions. Timely economic incentives as proposed can be very effective in offsetting the perceived cost of a female child. The proposals may be criticised as crassly materialistic by those who put their faith in education, awareness, empowerment of women and similar social interventions and a change in the mind-sets. A moral frame is no doubt relevant in the case of altruistic activities; as Titmuss demonstrated[6] fifty years ago, the system of voluntary donation of blood works much better and more effectively than the market solution of paying for blood. It appears, however, that in this situation of 'tragedy of the commons,' a moral 'framing' as advocated by the social reformers is unlikely to work.

## Endnotes

1 Dreze, Jean and Sen, Amartya, 2013, *An Uncertain Glory: India and Its Contradictions*, Allen Lane, Penguin Books, England.

2 Shermer, Michael, 2015, *The Moral Arc: How Science and Reason Lead Humanity Towards Truth, Justice and Freedom;* Henry Holt and Company, New York.

3 Wade, Nicholas, 2014, *A Troublesome Inheritance: Genes, Race and Human History*, The Penguin Press, New York, p. 158.

4 Jacquet, Jennifer, 2015, *Is Shame Necessary? New Uses for an Old Tool,* Allen Lane.

5 Lambsdorff, Johan Graf, 'Good Governance and the Invisible Foot' in Kerstin Kotschau and Thilo Marauhn (eds.) (2008), *Good Governance and Developing Countries,* Peter Lang Internationaler Verlog Development Wissenschaften Frankfurt.

6 Titmuss, Richard M., 1970: *The Gift Relationship: From Human Blood to Social Policy,* in (ed) Ann Oakley and John Ashton, The New Press 1997.

# 3

# Road Safety
## Regulatory 'Nudges' for Human Drivers

Road accidents kill more people than malaria or TB. The cost of road crashes has been assessed at one to two percent of GDP in the developed countries but the total costs, everything included—medical bills, lost output, vehicle damage etc.—may cost 10% of the GDP.[1] In India, the road fatality rate is 12.8 per lac of population and a study by the Planning Commission in 2002 estimated the social cost of road accidents at Rs. 55,000 crore (year 2000 prices) or about 3% of the GDP. Add to that the suffering, pain and trauma resulting from accidents which are difficult to quantify. The 80:20 rule holds with much more force in the case of road accidents; in Punjab, 82% of the fatalities in road accidents take place on a mere 4.79% stretch, mainly national highways and state highways, of the total road length. High speeds and alcohol are the main causes of a large percentage of accidents which happen mostly at the T-junctions and major crossings. Simply throwing more resources, manpower and regulations at the problem—tougher sentences, improvements in road design and construction, more training, more traffic police and so on—though necessary in many cases, may not be enough. Given the funding problems even for the maintenance of whatever infrastructure is available, it is unlikely that the government would have adequate resources for an ideal infrastructure, leaving aside the problems of space and other physical constraints. We need therefore to explore inexpensive options such as designing regulations which are compatible with the incentives and behaviour of the drivers.

## Static traffic offences

Traffic regulations cover both 'static' and 'moving' offences. Jumping lights, wrong parking, not wearing the seat belt etc. are static offences whereas the moving offences are violating the prescribed speed limits, use of mobiles, drunk-driving etc. Some welcome and behaviourally informed changes in the regulations covering static offences have occurred through a process of trial and error. One example is the provision for compounding of (most of) the traffic violations, a great convenience for the drivers. Compounding eliminates or at least reduces the temptation to offer a bribe if not to solicit it. Assuming that the cops' incentives are unchanged, this earlier implied that the drivers with out-of-state registration numbers had all the incentives to bribe the policeman in order to avoid transaction costs and the trouble and expense of making a visit again to appear in court and pay the fine. Considering that the compounding fees are not insignificant and the fact that humans are loss-averse, compounding is an effective strategy for securing compliance at minimum social cost.

Moreover, some of these norms, especially seat belts, have been socially accepted. There was initially some doubt about the efficacy of mandating seat belts. It was argued by some academics that this tended to encourage car drivers to take more risks. Landberg refers approvingly to Sam Peltzman's work in the mid 1970s and argues that safer driving equipment may lead to risky driving and more pedestrian deaths[2]! Whatever the truth, the rule is here to stay and having got general public endorsement, it has now become a habit or a social norm. One sits in the car and automatically clicks on the seat belt. Further, some other common violations such as jumping red lights will, in due course, be taken care of by technology and installation of scanning devices at the traffic junctions. Many countries have installed such equipment at the traffic junctions for automatic scanning of vehicles and recording the violations committed.

It may not be possible to prevent gaming of some of these rules. As Tyler Cowen[3] remarks, many markets are designed to help people avoid or circumvent regulations; he gives the example of a British entrepreneur selling 'squirt bottles of spray-on mud for licence plates' to circumvent the system of recording speed limit violations by the police cameras! Barring such innovative gaming of traffic regulations, compliance or even cognizance of the static offences may not require physical presence of a policeman once such digital devices are introduced. Thus the static offences, which are currently the focus of police operations, need not be a cause of worry in the long term. The main problems will continue to be high speeds and drunk drivers.

## High speeds/drunk driving

Head on collisions on main highways are now rare due to the road dividers separating the traffic lanes. Most of the accidents in the cities take place at the highway junctions and major crossings. The problem is aggravated in India by the diversity of vehicles—motor bikes, cycles, tractor trolleys and so on. Within the cities, fatal accidents mostly occur at night when the traffic is light and drivers tend to jump lights; this can be fatal when the two drivers approaching a crossing are under the same illusion—that there is no cross traffic! The problem areas are, and will probably continue to be, high speeds and drunk-drivers and mostly both in conjunction. Over-speeding is generally a compoundable offence but not drunk driving. Drunk driving (DUI or Driving Under Influence) is sought to be addressed through measures such as impounding of vehicles on the spot and a night in the police lock up for the driver but continues to be the main problem all over the world. Can more be done?

## Regulating rash drivers

Enforcement agencies face a dilemma in controlling high speed driving. Fixed cameras and speed scanners are subject to gaming by motorists who know about the location of the static scanning devices, can exercise restraint while approaching electronic scanners and then merrily keep on driving fast. This can be easily observed by a visitor to a European country such as Switzerland which relies primarily on unmanned fixed points for surveillance. On the other hand, ad hoc speed checks may be perceived mostly as 'luck of the draw' and, therefore, are rarely effective as deterrents; the offender blames his/her luck and carries on as usual! In India, ad hoc mobile speed checks are favoured over static monitoring devices common in the West. Policemen play the game of cleverly camouflaging the scanners whereas the drivers try to game these tactics by developing expertise in identifying such devices from a distance. I have heard that in some cities the location of these scanners and check-points is now flashed through the internet within the *whatsapp* groups. Thus neither the Western solution of fixed point scanners—designed to save manpower but subject to gaming—nor the home grown devious tactics seem very effective.

## Behavioural biases and tough regulations

One needs to remember that fines and punishments for over speeding have to be moderate enough not to provide perverse incentives for bribing the police and thus getting off lightly (recall the definition of self interest by Cialdini mentioned in *Introduction:* maximum gain at minimum cost). Given the factors indicated above and the rather low probability of a driver being caught over-speeding, the current regulations appear to have had a negligible effect especially as enforcement is also erratic. While the number of high speed drivers is rather large, only a few may be involved in or cause accidents and there is little chance therefore of negative reinforcement through fines and other penalties imposed on the 'other' drivers. Media reports of the accidents involving such *'other'* drivers may also not be enough to make the possibility of an accident salient or cognitively accessible to a driver. In any case the bias of 'over confidence' implies that no driver believes that he/she would cause an accident! And as behavioural economists have shown, while we tend to overestimate the probability of gain, the probability of loss (fine and punishment) is underestimated.

It is, therefore, unlikely that, given the present set of interventions, there will be much change or improvement in the rate of accidents. The traditional, though not time tested, administrative solution—harsher punishment—now under consideration by the Indian government to deter potential accident makers is unlikely to make a difference in the number of accidents or fatalities; just making the regulations more stringent does not appear to be enough.

## Regulatory compliance: a matter of 'Timing'

The road safety regulations need to be structured in the context of how and under what circumstances people tend to violate speed limits and/or drive under the influence of alcohol. And advances in behavioural sciences have provided enough evidence for what would work. Halpern[4] has coined an acronym EAST (Easy, Attract, Social, Time) for simple behavioural interventions. The last, Time, seems especially relevant in the case of rash and/or drunk driving. I remember having read about an experiment where different modes of punishment were designed for the dog-pups. In one variation, punishment (a mild slap) was administered just after the pups ate a piece of bread or cake (the temptation); the second variation provided for the punishment just before they attempted to do so. There was no change in the behaviour of pups in the first scenario; they whimpered at the punishment, probably felt guilty but back they came, repeated the action and got the same punishment. In the other case, the pups were successfully conditioned to avoid the temptation. We humans similarly need *ex-ante* or immediate cues to prevent actions, which are socially harmful but may be personally satisfying, to replace the regime of punishments and fines administered *post facto*, after the deed is done. An over speeding driver may not recall or visualize the consequences of his risky driving at the time he is driving—whether under the influence of emotions (teenagers racing against each other) or under the influence of alcohol/drugs; drivers need more salient and immediate cues and signals. Halpern points out[5] that conspicuous scanners installed in sensitive traffic zones (near accident prone crossings etc.), which alert drivers to be cautious, appear to have been effective, at least in the UK. A 'hide and seek' approach, as followed by the police in India, is not of much help in changing behaviour, though it may add to the quantum of fines or the personal kitty of the policemen.

Based on the work already done by the Nudge Unit and others, it appears that it would probably help if speed scanners are installed 100-200 metres *ahead* of the accident sites - accident prone crossings and dangerous stretches of roads known as the 'black spots'. Moreover, reflective and prominent signs which display the prescribed speed limits and flash signs, indicating to the errant driver that he/she is violating the speed limit, can be very effective. Such devices provide a signal or caution to the drivers *at the right time*, before their rash actions can cause damage.

## Speed governors: an effective mandate

If we are prepared to go beyond such 'nudges' to mandates and bans, the regulations could require that speed governors should be provided by the car manufactures; 100 Km hour for light motor vehicles could be considered a reasonable limit for this purpose whereas in the case of heavy vehicles, buses and trucks, it could be fixed at 80 Km hour. In fact, the law in India already provides for mandatory speed governors for heavy transport vehicles, though it is yet to be effectively enforced. This restriction on individual choice, though not very palatable to Richard Thaler and other practitioners and advocates of 'libertarian paternalism' (which is in favour of allowing people to make a socially productive choice through 'framing' the context and default rules), may be a small price to pay in the interest of reducing the number of accidents and fatalities. While data regarding a cause-effect relationship, if any, between high speeds and the frequency and intensity of accidents is not available, it appears a 'safe' guess that most of the serious accidents, which result in fatalities, take place when the vehicles involved are being driven at egregiously, rather than marginally, high speeds. On the National Highway connecting Punjab to Delhi, for example, over 90% of the vehicles can be observed being routinely driven at speeds of more than 120–130 kms hr most of the time, even though the prescribed speed limit is only 90 kms; and it is impossible to install scanners all along the roads.

A mandate for speed governors would not leave any scope, short of disabling the device, for rash driving. Enforcement of the regulation is also easy as the police have to only ensure that the speed governors, when checked, are functional. And surely, as economists never tire of saying, markets will emerge to provide private racing tracks for enthusiastic drivers trying out their Ferraris! The loss of satisfaction and thrill provided by high speeds to the few will be more than compensated by the huge social gains.

## Cognitive overload: over-supply of rules

There is a need to address another problem in India; this is the bewildering array of mandated speed limits which appear to be codified on an ad hoc basis without much study or research. In Chandigarh the variation in speed limits can range from 45 kms hr for some roads to 50, 55, 60, 65 kms for some others. And for mysterious reasons, heavy vehicles always have slightly more rigorous standards even when the mandated speed limits are rather low, 35-40 km hr, which may not even be the top gear speed. Considering the present speed-friendly design of vehicles and the expectation frame of the human drivers (imagine asking drivers to comply with a uniform but modest speed limit of 50 km only!), speed limits need to be realistic and *need to be so viewed by a majority of drivers.*

Sendhil Mullainathan mentions the problem of the limited 'cognitive band width' for the poor who have to cope with many problems[6]. It is difficult, not only for the poor but most of the humans, to make a rational choice if confronted with too many bytes of information, factors and options; it is then cognitively easier just to go by the intuitive System I. Motorists may develop a mental frame for ignoring speed regulations if they find it difficult to keep track of the variety and confusing clutter of speed limits, varying continually from 45 km on road A to 55 km on road B to 60 km on road C and so on. System 1 of the brain may not absorb such confusing information about the slightly varying thresholds notified for different roads and areas especially when a driver has many other things on his/her mind—impressing the first date, making a presentation to the boss, family problems etc.

These factors are no doubt somewhat trivial in comparison with those affecting the poor, as mentioned above, but nevertheless have similar consequences. Needless to add, the possibility of an accident is probably the last thing in mind of an over confident driver! A couple of variations, rather than a range of sophisticated calibrations, would probably do a better job. Moreover, the prescribed speed limits need to make sense to the drivers and should be neither too high to make accidents more likely, nor so low that most of the motorists ignore them. A set of reasonable 'anchors' could be—Highways 90 kms, urban areas 65 kms and other roads 70 kms; this may be more salient and easier for the drivers to recall. To use a term from the game theory, there will be less confusion about the 'focal point', thus making compliance easier. This strategy will also be sensible considering the high proportion of cars now available which are designed for instant acceleration and can drive comfortably at +120 km speed.

## Drunk driving: is a zero tolerance policy feasible?

In the case of drunk driving, one aspect that needs to be carefully evaluated is the prescribed blood alcohol concentration (BAC) threshold. A zero tolerance policy (no alcohol at all) does appear attractive but human nature and the seemingly pleasurable, though perverse, experience the alcohol intake provides, make it unlikely that tough standards of compliance will bring about the desired results.

Data regarding motor vehicle accidents caused by speeding vehicles driven by the DUI drivers is not readily available. For India even the data regarding the proportion of accidents caused by the highly inebriated drivers (say above .10 BAC) is not readily available. One can, however, speculate, as the data for the USA shows, that high levels of speed and alcohol would go together. Though the legal limit in the US is .08, there is a demand to lower it to .05. In India, the limit is rather low (.03). The proposal to make it more stringent is puzzling when the regulators in the West are struggling to achieve substantial compliance even at the much higher limits prescribed. Some dimensions of the problem of drunk driving can be seen from the following data for the USA.

(i) People drive DUI almost three hundred thousand times but fewer than 4,000 are arrested – a little over 1% (www.madd.org – Mothers Against Drunk Driving website).

(ii) Alcohol impaired driving accidents cause 31% of all traffic related deaths.

(iii) In 2012, over 1.3 million drivers were arrested DUI, this is just 1% of 121 million self reported episodes among the US adults annually.

(iv) Drugs are mostly used in combination with alcohol mostly by the young (www.cdc.org. – Centre for Disease Control and Prevention website).

(v) 85% of drivers involved in crashes with BAC of .01 or higher had a BAC of above .08 and 59% had BAC above .15 (www.rita.dot.gov – Bureau of Transportation Statistics).

Interventions such as sobriety check points have been effective but the limitation is that of resources. Some of the States in the US provide for Ignition Interlocks for convicted offenders – alcometres which ensure that a car would not start if the driver's BAC is above .08. These are reported to be quite effective (www.cdc.gov). What the data shows is the correlation of high BAC levels and fatal accidents.

## The case for moderation in the BAC levels

It may be prudent in India to have a limit which is a little more realistic, say .05 BAC, all aspects considered—causal relationship between high BAC and accidents, human nature and the common propensity to drink, may be not always in excess. This may also help in moderate drinking becoming a social norm, rather than the present limit of .03, which most of the people *who drink* may find completely unreasonable. There is little point in imposing BAC limits which 90% of the drivers *who drink* are likely to violate. Another problem with the rather low BAC threshold is that it may promote "what the hell" feeling; drivers who like a drink but find that even a small 30 ml shot is punishable, may throw caution to the winds; penalty would be the same whether the BAC is .04 or .08!

## Motivating (parents of) teenage drivers

Another intervention can be based on what is known in business as market segmentation—having a separate marketing strategy for different consumer groups and segments. One such major group is that of teenagers. It is known that unlicenced drivers especially teenagers are responsible for a large number of accidents. The number of accidents caused by unlicenced drivers has been rising; it went up by 54% from 2012 to 2014; more than half of these are caused by teenagers (www.*indpedia.com*). This category of teenagers who may be DUI, drive mostly at high speeds, but who are not even eligible for a licence under the law (+18 is the cut off age for four wheelers) may not respond to the common interventions of fines and jail. Their rash driving may even be a rational response to the Juvenile Justice laws which treat teenager crimes leniently, as Gary Becker may well argue[7]. *We need some strong cues not for the teenagers but for their parents.*

Some countries have Three or Four Strikes laws—the last such offence means automatic escalation of the prison sentence or no parole. Something similar would probably work in the case of unlicenced teenage drivers—or all unlicenced drivers for that matter. The rules should seek to influence the behaviour not of the teenager but the parents. Probably heavy fines and suspension of registration of the vehicle may do the trick. Impounding the vehicle driven by a teenager for a month or more may be quite effective in keeping the parents more watchful. Though we have no data, most of the teenagers probably drive vehicles with the connivance, if not the consent of their parents. Considering the reputation of police in the safe - keeping of impounded vehicles, this may be the way to go about addressing the problem of teenage drivers! In any case, this is better than the patently illegal and absurd proposal, to send the parents of an errant minor to prison, which is reportedly being 'seriously' considered by the Indian government!

## Change behaviour, not mindsets

Behavioural scientists differentiate the role and relevance of external and internal influences on behaviour and persuading people to adopt or refrain from a particular course of action or behaviour. In the case of government policy, most of the external influences—defined through rules and regulations—are punitive, whereas most of the encouragements and incentives are non material and show a pathetic dependence on the wishful probability of internal change among the drivers. Governance interactions cover whole populations and it is rarely possible for governments to focus resources on say an ideal school or a hospital or specific individuals or develop "islands of excellence". Dedicated NGOs are effective primarily because they have a specific and limited canvas, focus and charter. A cancer foundation for example will judge its efficiency by how many patients it has helped. An NGO can start its operation just with one village, as the Tilonia (Rajasthan) example shows. Governments don't have such freedom. It is difficult for them to bring about internal change among the citizens at large, given these constraints of having to provide for universal application of whatever interventions are decided. Governments need therefore to focus on external influences, signals and cues to influence behaviour. Second, while the trick is to make it easy for citizens to comply, the rules generally provide a liberal dose of material disincentives in the form of punitive regulations. If a day in the police lock-up does not seem to work, provide for a week's incarceration in prison for the inebriated driver! No doubt, it may not be possible to devise positive triggers, cues and nudges all the time but nudges and kicks are not mutually exclusive. One can design punitive rules for social conduct and behaviour and simultaneously support these by measures which make compliance easy. The measures listed above may be helpful in that direction.

Some simple and inexpensive additions and changes in the infrastructure and logistics of traffic can also help reduce accidents. Road safety can be improved by providing footpaths (84% have none), safe places for pedestrians to cross roads, central barriers to stop head on collusions, speed bumps at deadly junctions, fences between cars and pedestrians[8] and so on. Foot bridges need to be designed for the convenience not of drivers but pedestrians; most of the foot bridges may in fact force pedestrians to prefer risky road-crossings. Some basic safety features can also be made mandatory. The ABS (Anti-lock Braking System) and airbags are two simple components for safety especially the former. Behavioural interventions matter primarily because they are inexpensive, help in making safe driving a habit and need not cost any money and a bit of attention to the fallibility and vulnerability of human beings may pay high dividends. If we are to persuade the drivers to comply with restrictions on speed and consumption of alcohol, fines and sticks have to be supplemented by institutions, which make it easy and convenient for them to comply, which most of us consider reasonable and which we ourselves observe to be the social norm rather than a government dictate.

## Endnotes

1 *The Economist,* Reinventing the Wheel, January 25-31, 2014.
2 Landberg, Steven E., 1995/2009, *The Arm Chair Economist: Economics and Everyday Life,* Pocket Books, UK.
3 Tyler, Cowen, 2006, *Discover Your Inner Economist,* Dutton/Penguin Books.
4 Halpern, David, 2015, *Inside the Nudge Unit: How Small Changes Can Make a Big Difference,* W.H. Allen.
5 Halpern, 2015, Ibid.
6 Mullainathan, Sendhil and Shafir, Eldar 2013, *Scarcity: Why Having Too Little Means So Much,* Allen Lane/Penguin Books.
7 Becker, Gary S., 'Crime and Punishment: An Economic Approach', *Journal of Political Economy,* Vol. 76, No. 2 (March—April 1968, pp. 169–217). He argued that criminal acts and even addiction may be rational choices for addict and criminals.
8 *The Economist,* 2014, Ibid.

# 4

# Rules for Human Smokers and Drinkers

Alcohol and smoking are both addictive though the chemical properties and the nature of the 'high' are different. Government policies which mostly discourage consumption, as in the case of cigarettes, but sometimes even ban trade and consumption, as some states in India have done in the case of alcohol can benefit substantially from the insights and findings of behavioural sciences.

## I. Smoking

International experience indicates that in the case of smoking, the two measures which have been very effective are: (a) prices and (b) ban on smoking in public places. The later, as Halpern observes[1], has a multiplier effect; the social norm of not smoking in a public place is soon internalized by most of the smokers when they observe other smokers refrain from smoking. We are, however, still far from a smoke-free world. Price, the basic economic incentive, is a potent weapon. It is an important economic incentive and that is why cigarettes are subject to heavy taxation all over the world, including India. It is, however, a double-edged weapon; price can neither be too low—that would encourage smoking—nor too high, as that may create illegal markets for substandard or smuggled products or more dangerous substitutes. Supply will always appear from somewhere if there is demand for a product, as has been noticed in the case of narcotic drugs, and taxation, therefore, is a tightrope walk which needs to be carefully negotiated. These two interventions are generally supported by social marketing and display of graphic and disgusting images of the damage caused by smoking on the cigarette packs.

In the flurry of making tough regulations, we should not, however, forget the smokers and their weaknesses and the nature of temptation provided by a smoke. The problem is mainly the System 1 of the smoker as mentioned in *Introduction*. While my logical and deliberative System 2 may know the statistical probability of the damage caused by smoking, System 1 makes me confident that I personally will not be affected or harmed; we tend to underestimate the probability of loss or damage. A smoker is also well suited for the self-serving bias of under assessment of the risk of smoking. Then there is the well known tendency to procrastinate, especially when one has to get out of a bad habit: I will smoke today, may be leave it tomorrow, or wait for the next year for a new resolution and till then merrily smoke away!

## 'Nudging' smokers

The problem, therefore, is how to design regulations to 'nudge' human smokers, who are vulnerable to temptation and constantly harried by the 'monkey on their shoulder', to kick the habit. The battery of interventions mentioned above may need some reinforcements to help smokers in taking a decision which is emotionally as well as cognitively difficult. One of these is encouraging the consumption of harmless substitutes. Three possible substitutes for smoking are e-cigarettes, nicotine patches and nicotine chewing gums. These probably need to be promoted, or at least should not be discouraged, subject of course to safeguards about product quality and safety. Halpern has analysed[2] the pros and cons of e-cigarettes and rightly concludes they are any day better than cigarettes; they do not contain tar and other chemicals and do not have much nicotine either. In the case of nicotine gums, which contain nicotine in pure chemical form, low end products can be promoted. The currently available nicotine gums provide only two options, 4 mg. and 2 mg. I am not aware whether it is feasible but probably 1 mg. nicotine gum pack may be as, if not more, popular; it will cost less, is less addictive and easier to kick off. There is little harm in encouraging less harmful and safer substitutes especially when a complete ban on smoking is not politically and economically feasible. In any case, these substitutes should not be banned, as some states in India seem to be doing in the case of nicotine chewing gums. The logic behind such prohibitions is somewhat strange - that the gum contains nicotine and is addictive whereas it is meant precisely for assisting smokers to kick the habit of smoking! Coaches emphasise while training young golfers to 'change one thing at a time'. The target today should be cigarettes and tobacco. We can ban or nudge the consumption of e-cigarettes and nicotine gums later when we find these have become the problem instead.

## Banning the sale of loose cigarettes: is it a good idea?

One of the issues is whether loose cigarette sales should be banned. There is no evidence that availability of loose cigarettes in the market encourages smoking. Smaller packs (five cigarettes per pack) may in fact lead to reduced consumption; buying a full pack means more temptation and more consumption. As Sunstein suggests, switching from a 20 cigarette pack to a 10 cigarette pack may itself reduce consumption[3]. While more evidence is needed, it is only logical that loose cigarette sales should help reduce the quantity consumed, if not the number of smokers. Personal experience of smokers also supports this proposition. This is due not only to the disincentive of having to pay more for loose cigarettes but also the hassle of making many visits to the market and incurring extra transaction costs. In fact many smokers, who want to kick the habit or reduce smoking, do it through a *self commitment not to buy a full pack of cigarettes.*

Measures such as banning the sale of loose cigarettes therefore only make it more difficult for smokers to cut smoking. Governments need to make smoking 'in the present' more difficult by an appropriate 'choice architecture' by manipulating the factors of price and availability and encouraging self commitment by smokers.

## Chewing tobacco

In India, the problem of consumption of tobacco is more serious due to the ready availability of other alternative products. One is *bidi* (rolled leaf tobacco) smoking and the second is chewing tobacco or *zarda;* these are a poor person's substitutes for expensive cigarettes. The option of raising prices through heavy taxation is not available in the case of *bidis*—millions derive their livelihood from tobacco cultivation, trade and sales; and products such as *zarda* have become favourite substitutes as many families and children have started objecting to smoking by adults even in the privacy of their homes. Tobacco chewing, therefore, is in as a substitute as nobody notices it and the absence of smoke means there is little damage except to the consumer.

## Nudging zarda consumers to safer substitutes

A number of state governments have banned the sale of *zarda* or chewing tobacco but absolute bans don't seems to work as has been observed in the case of drugs. That is the reason most of the countries in the West are shifting towards legalising drugs such as cannabis which are considered less dangerous than opium and its derivatives. One problem with banning a product is that what is considered desirable (may be a short term kick or pleasure) may become more so if the same is made scarce or banned and this holds especially for the teenagers and the young. Cialdini devotes a chapter to the scarcity principle and how it helps create demand for the scarce product; call it the 'scarcity heuristic'. It will be unwise to ignore the human consumers and how they are likely to behave and/or to react. In the case of *beedis* and chewing tobacco, the only feasible intervention seems to be to encourage affordable substitutes which are not harmful, at least not to that extent. One possible substitute is *pan masala*. Toxic properties of *pan masala* which does not contain tobacco need to be examined by experts to decide whether it can be promoted as a safer substitute by providing appropriate incentives through taxes, of course after defining the safety specifications, if necessary. Then there is the universal and harmless substitute, the chewing gum; the problem is that while this is a cost-effective option for the developed economies, it may not fit the budget of most of the consumers in India at the current prices.

## Social norms marketing: graphic images on cigarette packs

The strategy of marketing of social norms and highlighting the dangers of smoking through a graphic display of disgusting images of damaged lungs, mouth or throat, supported by similar advertisements, is now being increasingly used. There is no doubt that pictorial warnings are more effective than text messages; they convey the message even to illiterate, and are known to add to the motivation to quit smoking. The messages, however, need to be carefully designed. Images on the front of the pack matter more than those on the back. Further, while these graphic pictures are useful for educating smokers and others about risks, they may not help them in quitting smoking and even graphic images are subject to wear out over time[4].

There has been some debate in India about the space to be covered by such displays. Aggressive advocacy groups want over 80% of the cigarette pack to be covered in place of the current 40%. It seems that proponents of a heavy psychological kick, through disgusting images covering almost the entire pack, have won, but it is likely to be a pyrrhic victory. While graphic ads are intended to create feelings of disgust, smokers may not even notice them, once they get accustomed to seeing them every day[5]; familiarity is very likely to breed neglect and indifference, if not contempt. Probably the only effective cue, were it possible, will be a laser image of the damaged lungs projected on to the clouds of the cigarette smoke exhaled by the smokers! Governments also need to be careful about causing 'reactance', people's negative reaction to the efforts to control or restrict them; overdoing such actions may sometimes lead to defiance[6].

We do need to harness the potential and power of social norms, but first we have to create these norms, as mentioned in the case of income tax (Chapter 5). The first step in a strategy for social proof is to turn the current majority of the deviant consumers into a minority — whether the number of smokers in this case, or of drunken car drivers in the case of road safety (Chapter 3). This has been achieved to some extent through a ban on smoking in public places as indicated above. Unfortunately, though there is more than enough by way of social reproof and disapproval, the current policy provides little support for social proof. This practice needs to be reversed. The government needs to reinforce the social norms by highlighting how the number of smokers has come down over time, rather than bemoaning that the policy is not making enough impact. People tend to 'overestimate the prevalence of undesirable behaviours and use their perception as a standard against which to compare their own behaviour'. Under-graduates in a university reduced their alcohol intake when they were informed about the actual pattern of consumption of alcohol—that students consume less alcohol than what was thought to be the norm.

In the later part of the 20th century, as Gladwell mentions, psychologists such as Eyesenck used to focus on the 'smoker personality', his/her genetic predisposition to smoking and how treatment of depression, to which smokers were believed to be prone, could itself impact the urge to smoke[7]. He also mentions that by and large, most of the moderate smokers (five cigarettes a day) may not consume enough nicotine to get addicted. Such sophisticated approaches appear to be difficult because it is rarely possible for any government to devise selective policies for diverse consumers and groups. In the case of smoking, however, it can devise separate strategies as indicated, for the two very distinct groups of addicted smokers and the new recruits to their ranks, keeping in view their specific weaknesses and vulnerabilities.

## II. Alcohol

As in the case of smoking, alcohol consumption patterns are also very distinctive in India. We have a large variety— imported, IMFL (India Made Foreign Liquor), country liquor and, of course, illicit liquor, with an extensive range of prices. Heavy taxes are not an easy option especially as the levy of excise duties on alcohol is a state prerogative and a major source of revenue for them. Moderation rather than elimination needs to be the objective here. The policy of levying excise duties and taxes on the basis of alcohol content, irrespective of quality, does not make sense from this perspective. For example, beer laced with alcohol is allowed to be marketed as beer because one can label as an alcoholic beverage whatever catches the fancy provided excise duties are paid *according to the quantity of alcohol in the product.*

Three policy interventions can be very effective: standardisation, promoting smaller size bottles and cans, and low-alcohol drinks. Molasses based alcohol can be marketed today as whisky or even brandy whereas these should be cereal based and grape based respectively as per generally agreed standards. Indian regulators are not bothered about the concepts of maturity and ageing which is internationally the main marker of quality for hard drinks; consumers are entitled to know whether they are drinking vodka or whisky or beer or wine. There is thus need for a basic level of standardisation of the alcohol based products. Surprisingly, while whole pages of the *Food Safety and Standards Act* in India are devoted to specifications of milk, cheese and similar products, leaving the informal sector producers and vendors befuddled, I could not find more than a couple of lines in the Act on alcoholic beverages. This omission is surprising as even the product itself is not very safe, not to speak of its adulteration, and the industry is highly organised which makes it much easier to regulate!

## Promoting small size bottles and cans

It is well known that people are not rational in their consumption habits, especially for products such as alcohol and so on. How much is consumed, of coffee or beer, depends on the size of the can and bottle. A half-pint of beer may be enough for a common customer if offered as a default in place of a one-pint mug. Eliminating or heavily taxing the 650 ml. bottle for beer and promoting smaller size bottles for beers and whiskies may itself lead to reduced consumption. Further, studies show that people eat more when the portion size is large, whether popcorn buckets or bagels or sandwiches[8]. Consumption of whisky similarly depends a lot on whether the standard or default serving is a 30 ml drink or a 60 ml drink.

Low alcohol drinks

People who have consumed absolute alcohol (over 150% LP), tell me that they tend to consume the same quantity of absolute alcohol that they habitually consume, even though the usual hard drinks have only half the volume ($75^0$ LP). Low volume alcohol drinks can be promoted to encourage moderation in consumption. Country liquor is now generally sold at 50% LP (London Proof) strength as against 75% LP, the universal minimum for hard drinks. Governments could consider promoting low alcohol (40% LP) distilled liquor as in the case of low alcohol beers by levying excise duty at lower rates. *Duties and taxes thus can be structured to shift preferences to more desirable alternatives such as wine/beer/country liquor containing moderate percentage of alcohol.*

Businessmen exploit human weakness by discounting large cups of coffee or double-decker ham-burgers. Government need to use this very strategy but for discouraging consumption. Encouraging low alcohol drinks and smaller size can and bottles can be a very effective combination; both reduce consumption—smaller portions and bottles by limiting consumption and low alcohol drinks by giving the impression that one is consuming more than one should. Duties and taxes can thus be used to provide an appropriate 'choice architecture' to shift the pattern of alcohol consumption.

Theodore Roosevelt (as Commissioner of Police, New York in the late 1890s) banned the sale of whisky on Sundays except for hotels/restaurants. This led to the pubs and bars becoming hotels overnight with make-shift dingy rooms in their lofts and soggy sandwiches for food. The ban led to a new manifestation of prostitution even in places which earlier provided only alcohol! The experience of Prohibition in the US is a well known example of the failure of drastic bans and mandates. Governments would do well to consider the human smokers and consumers of alcohol while devising institutions and rules for changing their behaviour. Absolute bans and restrictions on consumption and sale are not enough; we need to help people kick off these bad habits by encouraging the sale of small size packs and containers and of course loose cigarettes and less harmful substitutes. In these areas what Halpern calls 'radical incrementalism'[9] is much more likely to work: "dramatic improvements can be achieved ..... by systematically testing small variations in everything we do rather than through dramatic leaps in the dark; improving small components of a programme or intervention leads to a dramatic improvement in performance and outcomes."

## Endnotes

1 Halpern, David, 2015, *Inside the Nudge Unit: How Small Changes Can Make a Big Difference*, p.133, W.H. Allen.
2 Halpern, 2015, Ibid.
3 Sunstein, Cass R, 2013, *Simpler: The Future of Government*, Simon and Schuster ebook
4 *Bulletin of the WHO 2009*, The impact of pictures on the effectiveness of tobacco warnings, www.who.int.
5 Halpern, 2015, Ibid.

6 Sunstein, 2013, Ibid.
7 Gladwell, Malcolm, 2000/2010, T*he Tipping Point: How Little Things can Make a Big Difference*, Abacus.
8 National Center for Chronic Disease Prevention and Health Promotion, Research to Practice Series No. 2, May 2006. www.cdc. gov
9 Halpern, 2015, Ibid.

# 5
# Income Tax Law
## Changing the Default Settings

The two major revenue earners for the Indian government are income tax (levied by the Central Government but shared with the states) and sales tax or VAT which at present is the state prerogative. Income tax regulations have been simplified and are by and large easy to comply. The GoI (Government of India) has taken a number of steps to make life easy for the tax payer—quick refunds, restrictions on appeals against decisions favourable to private parties, simplifying the tax forms, e-filing etc. The Income Tax department is probably much ahead of other tax agencies in this respect but it does not seem to have been very successful in its main charter—reducing the gap between the revenue potential and its realisation. It is difficult to estimate the revenue foregone through tax avoidance or tax evasion but both of these problems continue to bother the Indian government. One take on taxes is idealistic—that taxes are actually debts owed to government (and that tax payers should so view it!) and need to be used for redistribution. The possibility, however, of tax payment becoming pleasurable is rather remote and the department needs to focus on optimising revenues even while ensuring that taxes cause minimum resentment.

## Behavioural interventions in the Indian context

Halpern[1] has listed a number of behaviour-based interventions such as providing social proof that most of the people pay taxes (the claim however has to be true) and changing the design of e-mail reminders to encourage timely filing of Returns. Of course economists can always to suggest more rational slabs and tax rates. Such interventions, which may be appropriate in the context of the UK, are unlikely to work in India. Take the strategy of providing 'social proof', by informing people about the (high) %age of people who do pay taxes. The claim may not be true in India and the people know it; the current perception is that only the salaried employees pay the tax and all the others—corporates, self employed professionals, trade and business—mostly avoid or evade income tax and on the other hand have been gifted with massive rebates.

The pressure not surprisingly, therefore, on the Indian government is to raise the taxable-income limits, lower the tax rates and provide more and more exemptions year after year for the large number of 'honest' tax-payers. The general belief is that these measures are necessary for creating a level playing field for the two categories of citizens—those who pay taxes honestly (the salaried class) and others who evade them or manage substantial concessions. Further, it is difficult to sell the budget proposals for raising tax slabs and rates as the current tax rates function as the reference points and 'anchors' and additional taxes encounter strong public resentment due to 'loss- aversion'; a loss of Rs. 100 may equal a gain of Rs. 200-250 in terms of psychological impact. It is therefore more and more difficult to raise the targeted revenue from the limited number (reportedly 38 million) of tax payers out of which around 30% claim refunds. The silver lining is that with inflation, the same tax rates will net more revenue even without any change in the tax rates; it is difficult to impose salary cuts but employees rarely notice virtual cuts when inflation erodes wages.

## Making sense of 2016–17 tax proposals

The income tax proposals in the 2016–17 Budget of the Government of India contain a number of proposals which are interesting when considered from a behavioural perspective. The first is a proposal to levy tax on 60% of the savings corpus, such as the PPF (Public Provident Fund) etc., at the time of withdrawal. No doubt, there is some logic in taxing withdrawals at the final stage especially when the first two stages, of deposit and accumulation of the corpus, are exempt but the proposal is not really sustainable, has understandably led to a big uproar and resentment, and has been withdrawn. In any case, it was unlikely to achieve its purpose of making the pension schemes more attractive. It is not very wise to expect that the savers, while taking a decision today, whether to opt for a pension or a savings scheme, will be influenced by the possibility of *losses in the remote future*; this is standing the bias of hyperbolic discounting on its head!

The proposals however will be more saleable and create less resentment if only the withdrawals effected before the age of 60 years were to be taxed and at somewhat lower rates; that will give an option to individuals to plan their retirement funds as they wish, as pension/annuity, or as corpus to be invested, even while providing a disincentive for others who make early withdrawals. In fact pension schemes can be made attractive not by making incentives available in the remote future but in the 'present', at *the time people decide where to save and invest*. At present, all the savings schemes, including pensions, are given the same concessional treatment of full rebate upto a maximum of

Rs. 1.5 lac only per annum. The only additional incentive for the NPS (National Pension Scheme) is that an additional saving of Rs. 50,000/ can get you a further rebate. The problem is that for most of us it may be difficult even to save Rs. 1.50 lac and the role of the proposed incentive for the NPS is, therefore, very likely to be marginal. A better way will be to provide more attractive incentives for pension schemes, such as the NPS, by providing a tax rebate say at 150% of the NPS saving, as compared to 100% exemption for other saving schemes.

The second proposal is about tax rate reductions which may get media attention but are rarely noticed; people tend to discount marginal gains (but not losses). Tax payers did not even notice the reduced tax liability (by Rs. 3,000) announced for tax payers in the Rs. 5 lac income bracket. It does not appear to be a good strategy to extend further concessions; it is almost impossible to get back on track and withdraw such concessions later due to the phenomenon of an exaggerated psychological perception of loss.

## Presumptive tax: a default rule with no takers

The proposal for a presumptive tax for professionals (they can now pay presumptive tax on 50% of the total income in case such income does not exceed Rs. 50 lacs) is an interesting illustration of a default rule; an assessee has the option to claim more rebate/pay less tax provided detailed accounts are maintained. It is expected that this measure will encourage many defaulters to come into the tax net but the expectation is unlikely to be fulfilled. The threshold—treating 50% of income as taxable—is not very attractive. Tax advisors feel that the limit of 50% is rather high and probably a presumptive tax on 40% of income would have been more attractive as a default option; and the limit could always be revised in the light of the experience and the number of persons opting for it.

In fact Indian government had made similar attempts in the past but without much success. A system of presumptive tax was initiated in the 1990s for roping in the informal business sector—if I remember the tax was only Rs. 1,400 per annum. There were no takers and the new versions thereof (8% presumptive tax) do not seem to be doing any better. *The Report on Presumptive Direct Taxation 1995* by the NIPFP (National Institute of Public Finance and Policy) recommended a number of steps (e.g. field surveys) for promoting this option, but the response was not encouraging. In fact the paradox is that very few small businesses accepted this option whereas the rich diamond trade wants to be covered under this provision as per newspaper reports!

Presumptive tax is a sort of default rule under which one pays 8% tax on the turnover without having to maintain accounts etc. but this simple default means a definite loss of that 8% for a business *which may otherwise pay nothing at all*. Obviously very few choose the option. Inertia and status quo bias is reinforced by the known behavioural trait of loss aversion and there is little by way of a social norm to turn the tide. The problem is that a substantial majority are defaulters and penal provisions are unlikely to help when the target group is a huge mass of citizens most of whom are defaulters.

## Designing rules for improving the tax base

The main concern of the government has to be to widen the tax base to get out of the trap of high taxes on a limited base, accompanied by more and more concessions. The *Economic Survey 2015-16* mentions that only 5% of the adult earners are paying tax at present whereas at least 23% should; this means a five-fold increase in the number of tax payers and that may not happen if the traditional approaches are continued. Persons having income upto

Rs. 2.5 lac are exempted at present from filing Income Tax Returns and salaried employees need not file it in case of income below Rs. 5 lac. Considering that income tax is payable by individuals rather than families, one should expect around 10-15 crore individuals and self employed businesses to file tax returns even though all of them may not be liable to or actually pay the tax. A different approach could be more fruitful—focus on increasing the number of persons who file returns which may lead to more tax revenues in due course. *The department needs to orient its strategy to first expand the base of those who file Returns rather than trying to leapfrog straightaway to a wider tax base. A smart mix of positive nudges and negative incentives can possibly be worked out for adding to the number of people filing tax returns.*

## 'Nudges' for optimizing tax returns

The first step is making it easy and convenient to file a Tax Return, may be by providing 'free' service of the 'tax preparers' for businesses which do not file Returns at present and by promising acceptance of the Return at face value at least for a couple of years. In other words, the department accepts whatever the income declared. The psychological journey then of a trader or a professional, from the 'inertial' stage of filing a mandatory Return, without any obligation to pay the tax, to the destination of tax payment, may be a little more smooth and acceptable.

Some other mild mandates can be structured for most of the potential tax payers in business. The requirement of filing Returns is based on net income, whether salary earners or business. The problem is that in the case of trade and business the net income is a derived figure and it is hardly in any business's interest to voluntarily file the Returns and thus bell the cat. Fortunately one other objective but indirect indicator of the likely income is business turnover which is the basis for registration under the state

VAT/Sales Tax/Service Tax. All the registered dealers file VAT tax returns which also indicate the business turnover. The regulations could mandate income tax Returns, say, for all the registered dealers with a Rs +5 lac turnover. It is difficult to find fault with this measure as, unlike the levy of presumptive tax, only a Return is to be filed and the payment of tax depends on the net income or profits indicated by the accounts. Once businesses start filing tax returns, motivated by the mild incentives mentioned above, combined with possible adverse consequences if they don't, they may not react that violently when, after a few years, the taxman appears to scrutinize the Returns. The act of filing the Return would have mentally prepared the businesses for this eventuality.

Obviously that by itself may not be enough. The person or business knows that the relief is temporary and may not be willing to risk filing a Return. His/her System 2 and the calculating and rational self may worry more about the future than the ease of filing the Return in the present. The threat therefore of adverse consequences for defaulters who do not comply has to be more salient. While a generalized country-wide campaign may not help, suppose that the 'nudging' operations were to be made city/local area specific and were to be combined with the threat of *suo motu* surveys by the tax department after the window for filing Returns is closed. Special tax teams could be assigned this responsibility for a few major cities to be covered by rotation—how many and with what potential depends on the resources the department has for this purpose. The campaign can be supported by suitably designed local ads which promote the benefits and also the 'stick'; that after the window is closed, a detailed survey will be undertaken. *The route for marketing the social norm of tax payment in the case of businesses and professionals seems to lie through tax Returns.*

Localized campaigns for building the base of Returns, leading in due course to that of tax revenues, are likely to be more effective than warnings, patriotic appeals or expecting citizens to pay presumptive taxes when they know that there is little probability of a particular unit being picked up for scrutiny. Localized campaigns are likely to work much better as the clientele is limited and local, and the shoves and nudges are much more visible and salient. Further, the push given by a few who start filing returns can drive the evidence of 'social proof' and result in better compliance. The department would do well to initiate some pilots and moderate the suggested mix of incentives and communication strategies in the light of experience.

Other targets groups, such as the professional self employed etc., who are registered and/or pay service tax, can be similarly selectively covered in due course, depending on the potential and prospects as viewed by the department. In this case also, the prescribed threshold for filing the mandatory Returns can be in terms of turnover; the turn over data is available with the state sales tax department in the case of businesses and the Tax Department for service tax.

## Designing 'sticky' messages

There is a need also to redesign the messages and ad campaigns of the tax department. The present practice is to appeal to patriotism by roping in popular film actors and to highlight the social appeal of tax payment by holding functions to honour tax payers. Considering the present perceptions, social recognition of the top tax payers is unlikely to make a difference; high end tax payers, especially film stars, are widely perceived to be evading taxes. Another recently adopted practice is publicizing the names of big defaulters, *but publication of the list of defaulters may only reinforce the common perception — that big wigs evade taxes and are none the worse for it.*

*Probably a more effective protocol will be to publicize widely the list of big cases/persons who are successfully penalized for various violations.* Such information may be especially effective and salient if focussed at local/regional levels. One has just to see the negligible effect on the public of the list of Indian citizens having accounts in tax havens; *the practice of 'naming and shaming' in the Indian context is likely to succeed if it is directed not at the big defaulters generally but only those who have been successfully punished/prosecuted.*

The pre-requisite for increasing the tax base is increasing the base of income tax Returns and appropriate regulatory nudges need to be designed for this purpose. As mentioned, the psyche of a businessman at present is that avoidance and evasion is the norm. This is also possibly true. Once the defaulters become a minority, the strategies mentioned above — telling people that a substantial majority pay taxes or at least file Returns — are likely to be more effective.

Many liberals fear that behavioural insights will be used by the governments for manipulation. As Akerlof et al[2], however, emphasise, this is done by businesses all over the world (they call it 'phishing equilibrium') and there is nothing to prevent governments, if they wish, to do so even now. What is more likely is that government revenues will increase and the resistance to pay taxes will become weaker, once the tax department shift its sights from ham handed regulations and focuses on 'what works'[3].

## Wealth tax and death duties: a behavioural perspective

Wealth tax in India is on the statute books but the number of tax payers is negligible whereas inheritance taxes were abolished about thirty years back. Governments generally tend to consider the two taxes similarly, as if they were subject to similar client reactions and responses. In fact they are very different if viewed from a behavioural perspective. Wealth tax is difficult to sustain for the same reasons as a tax on income. It is a present and immediate loss for the taxpayer and any loss matters much more psychologically than its nominal value. Inheritance tax, however, is payable after death and very few people especially the super-rich may be bothered about what happens to their wealth after they die. It is therefore a very pragmatic tax, provided the concerns of the common man, in this case, the middle class, who are rightly worried about leaving their wives, husbands and children in modest comfort if they can do so, are addressed by exemptions. In India, for example, we could have a threshold of Rs. 50-100 crore at today's prices for levying estate duties. This will affect only 10% of the individuals who probably own 90% of the private wealth in the country and thus satisfy the tax revenue targets.

Kahneman refers[4] to the Swiss Scientist Daniel Bernoulli who in the late 1730s formulated the theory of the expected utility of wealth based on its diminishing utility in psychological terms. A loss of 1 million out of a 100 million wealth is very different from the same loss when the total wealth itself is only 2 million. The advantage of an inheritance tax directed at the super-rich is that most of them don't even know their total wealth especially when it is held in shares; a government can therefore afford to ignore the customary 'noise'. Another advantage is that such taxes are calculated on the total assets before the legal or natural heirs possess them, the latter don't own the property and so may not have the feelings associated with the loss of something owned, known as the "endowment effect".

Both of these taxes are partly redistributive taxes, which can be justified by considerations of equity alone, but inheritance taxes are more marketable. After all, the progeny of an Ambani or Bill Gates has little justification in expecting to inherit the wealth of their parents to which they have made little contribution. While estate duties and taxes will make a Thomas Piketty[5] happy, there won't be much by way of social loss, and this can be done without pushing the heirs as some would propagate, to the Raulsian level of justice.

It would seem that the Income Tax department in India can devise appropriate institutions and rule structures to make it easier for people to psychologically accept the painful fact of paying out taxes:

(a) Providing for mandatory Returns for businesses and professionals, based on turnover and not profits or net income.

(b) Levy of estate duties and inheritance tax rather than wealth tax on the super rich

(c) Social norms marketing focussed not on the high tax-payer role models, but on the *penalised big defaulters.*

(d) Timing the incentives for promoting pension schemes

## Endnotes

1 Halpern, David, 2015, *Inside the Nudge Unit: How Small Changes Can Make a Big Difference*, W.H. Allen.
2 Akerlof, A and Schiller, Robert J., 2015, *Phishing for Phools: The Economic of Manipulation and Deception*, Princeton University Press.
3 Halpern, 2015, Ibid.
4 Kahneman, Daniel, 2011, *Thinking Fast & Slow*, Farrar, Straus & Giroux, New York.
5 Piketty, Thomas, 2014 (Translated by Arthur Goldhammer), *Capital in the Twenty-First Century*, The Belknap Press/Harvard University Press.

# 6

# Crime Control
## Guarding the Guardians

International agencies such as the World Bank and The Transparency International regularly publish country rankings on corruption and governance. India is the biggest democracy but appears to fare no better than many African countries though we may be consoled that we are generally ahead of Pakistan and Afghanistan. Governance problems concern outcomes and social and economic indicators such as sanitation, health, literacy, poverty, as well as processes—transparency, equity, rule of law, ease of doing business. The issue considered here is that of law and order, with focus on crime, its prevention and control, and how a behavioural approach can improve outcomes. This is one area where, as will be seen, we need to be as, if not more, concerned about the motives and behaviour of the police, as the criminals.

## Popular themes of police reforms: Malimath Committee Report

Crime control is generally discussed in terms of macro and structural constraints on police functioning: inadequate strength, frequent transfers, faulty deployment (for non professional, meaning personal and household, duties) of even the limited number of policemen available, corruption, lack of autonomy etc. The Malimath committee[1] on reforms of the criminal justice system, which has made a number of recommendations covering major aspects of the criminal justice system, reflects this bias in favour of structural, organisational and administrative aspects of governance but appears to neglect the dimensions of interest, motivation and incentives of the actors involved. Some of the committee's recommendations for helping victims could even add to the perverse incentives of, and misuse by, the police. One example is the recommendation that there should be no distinction between cognizable and other offences and police should have the power to undertake investigation in all cases. This is suggested ostensibly to save the victim the bother of having to approach a magistrate directly for relief/justice. While this may facilitate quick redress and justice in the case of non-cognisable offences, (assuming we expect the police to provide justice, despite all evidence to the contrary), it would further add to the workload of the police—more pending cases—and possibly also to exploitation by the police, even in the case of offences now mercifully out of their grip. Similarly, the system of compensation recommended for the victims is not likely to help control crime; it will simply be an extension of the 'welfare state' philosophy to the victims of crimes. Some suggestions of the Committee such as entrusting investigation of serious crimes to the senior most police officer in the police station are likely to fare no better; professionalism and integrity is not necessarily the monopoly of seniors in hierarchy. Mafia-police nexus is leveraged mostly by the top officials.

Proposals of the Committee for liberalising the legal provisions for compounding appear to be well intentioned but the suggestion, that social/public interest should be the criterion for compounding, appears misconceived. As indicated later, it would be more appropriate to seek the rationale of these provisions in a satisfactory closure for the victim/family, rather than social good or social efficiency which is rather vague, difficult to define and liable to be misused.

No doubt proposals, such as having a broadly acceptable level of staff, reasonable autonomy and so on, are important for police functioning, but that is just the beginning of the story of failure. Chandigarh UT, Punjab and Delhi have some of the highest police-population ratios in India but this factor does not translate into improved crime statistics. If an econometric analysis were to be conducted for India, it will probably not indicate even a positive correlation. In any case, enough evidence is available globally and especially in the US, and as John R. Lotte Jr., an economist, observes,[2] 'run of the mill' administrative solutions—more staff, tougher laws—seem to make little difference in police effectiveness. James Q Wilson, one of the architects of the Broken Windows approach has remarked[3] on the futility of adding more and more judges to cope with increased work load, a favourite solution generally proposed in India to address the problem of case overload in Courts; the same is probably true of the staffing solutions to the problem of governance *by* the police.

## Best Practices: the NIH bias

Best practices tend to fade away. Soft interventions such as the experiment in community policing in Tiruchy district in Tamil Nadu taken up 20 years back[4] is now forgotten and new models such as *Janmaithri Suraksha* in Kerala have been introduced. The process of putting the old wine of ideological solutions in new bottles continues unabated. Ben Ramalingam has termed this pathology as 'best practicitis'[5]. The reason probably is 'Not Invented Here' (NIH) syndrome, as behavioural economist Ariely explains[6]: Thomas Edison, inventor of the light bulb and the DC (Direct Current) could not accept the fact that the AC (Alternating Current) technology of his competitor Tesla was superior. One reason, as I had explained in *Governance Unbound,* is that, unlike the private sector, there is little competition among governments and therefore little incentive to overcome the NIH bias.

## Motives, behaviour and crime

The 'Broken Windows'[7] approach mentioned earlier was formulated by Wilson and Kelling; according to this, police need to give priority to controlling minor crimes like breaking of glass windows by street hoodlums, to create a sense of order and thus prevent or reduce major crimes; ensuring that graffiti on the metro rail in New York was cleaned up immediately appears have contributed to a reduction in major offences on the rail network. The solution has its limitations; as Tim Harford (*The Undercover Economist*) has shown, the decline phase in the New York crime started *before* William Bratton took over as the Police Commissioner and applied the approach to the New York crime scene. John Lotte, referred above, conclusively demonstrates that most of the popular theories of crime control—community policing, broken windows, staff, gun control laws, mixed police force, abortion laws etc.—were not relevant to decline in crime in the 1990's in the USA. The relevant factors, according to him, were increased use of death penalty, rising arrest and conviction rates and the passage of right-to-carry law; enforcement in the key, as he remarks.

Strategies mandating more and more severe punishments, which are expected to provide more effective deterrence, appear to ignore the 'over confidence bias', that most of the human beings—including criminals—overrate their abilities. Death penalty or life imprisonment may not deter a criminal who is over confident of his ability to escape the law. The character of Don played by Shahrukh Khan in the Bollywood film *Don 2* is a fictional example of the mindset of many criminals; he is confident he can execute his plans perfectly without incurring adverse consequences. Criminals are also as likely as other humans to underrate the risk of arrest and punishment due to myopia and an appetite for risk for immediate gain, utility or gratification. They may not, therefore, be very rational in assessing the risk and the probability of arrest/jail and may heavily discount the loss of liberty in the remote future when the gains from crime are available in the immediate present. And in India, as is well known, the wheels of justice grind slowly and the rates of conviction are low.

One common problem with various crime control measures seems to be a lack of appreciation of the incentives of the government actors, the police in this case. Wilson, referred above, has defined the culture and character of different government agencies in terms of observability and concreteness of the tasks they perform and the outcomes they are responsible for. Police, according to him, is a 'coping' organisation, with tasks which are ill defined and difficult to measure; it is also subject to a lot of 'contextual constraints' (e.g. rights of the accused). Considering these difficulties, the rules also need to address the incentives and motives of the police, apart from those of criminals and the accused.

## Regulating police 'games'

A victim is not recognised under law as a stakeholder in the case of cognisable offences. Once the FIR is registered, what matters till the stage of prosecution is behaviour of the police and the accused. In a Kannada movie, *Beli Matthu Hola* (*The Fence and The Crop*) directed by PR Ramdas Naidu, the police extract money from the complainant, a moneylender who mortgages gold ornaments for loans to farmers), for registering an FIR regarding the theft of gold and other valuables. Later, the police even contemplate registering an FIR *against him* by inciting the farmers, who had mortgaged gold ornaments with the moneylender, to file a complaint that the moneylender himself had orchestrated the theft and defrauded the farmers! The situation is thus ripe for a win-win situation for the two parties left in the game - the criminal and the police. The former has to share only a part of the gains with the latter for both to be much better off. The victim does not figure in crime detection or prosecution except as a casual witness, may be, and the fiction probably falls even a little short of reality. The situation is therefore very different from what happens in socio economic exchanges, where we have the customer or the client, worker or the defrauded citizen, to aggressively follow up the matter in his or her interest. In North India, it is quite common for the police to accept or at least expect to get a bribe of Rs. 1-5 lac *just for registering an FIR* in matters which may essentially be civil disputes - violation of patents, alleged second sales of property on the basis of allegedly fraudulent power of attorney documents. The FIR registration is not an automatic but an extractive process; the complaint received is simply a trigger to extend the frontiers of exploitation rather than justice.

## FIR: report and registration

There are a number of areas where a simple tweaking of rules to factor in the incentives of the interacting parties may pay rich dividends. In case of police, one such 'nudge' or mild incentive can be to pin the responsibility for the *contents of the FIR register*– the initial stage of interaction of the actors - on the police, rather than allowing the victims to be used as a proxy and front for whatever the police wish to record and who they want to implicate. *The law and the system of registering an FIR assumes that what is reported and what is recorded in the FIR register can be different.* Complainants are not expected to be familiar with different sections of the Indian Penal Code (IPC) or the detailed clauses and sub sections and are not equipped to structure their complaints to fit particular sections of the IPC. Complaints are in practice got rewritten from complainants, complete with a listing of sections and clauses or at least the technical ingredients of the offence.

*This manipulation is possible as there is no system of keeping a factual and separate record of the complaint as distinct from its registration as an FIR.* Complaints made on telephone or given orally are not put on tape/videographed. One major reform from a behavioural perspective is therefore a mandatory requirement for a recording/videography of this initial interaction between the person reporting and the front desk recording the information or the complaint. This will encourage victims/complainants to orally communicate, or write down, the facts as they perceive them; now a missing person report can be registered as a kidnapping and a suspected kidnapping as a missing person report. The Supreme Court had to issue orders recently that reports about missing children must be registered as FIRs irrespective of what the parents report or the police feel appropriate; the reason was that such complaints were rarely registered as kidnapping cases. The current system of recording and registration of the FIRs thus mostly suits the police and their incentives, whether for favourable crime statistics, extraction of bribes or whatever.

The police station *needs to own what is recorded in the FIR register*, as distinct from the complaint or information received under Section 154 of the Cr.PC, which in its spontaneous form has to be owned by the complainant;

and evidence of the interaction—oral or written—needs to be preserved in all cases so that it can be accessed for verification in case the FIR is suspected to be manipulated or delayed or differs in material particulars from the complaint. In fact, the concept of *zero FIR*, now mostly used for offences against women, is a step in that direction as the process of registration is moved away from the domain of the investigating police station. And that is why it is unlikely to become a standard practice, unless the Cr.PC rules are suitably changed. *The FIR is today being treated less as information and more as evidence; the very first step after registration in most of the cases is for the police to proceed to make an arrest even without a semblance of investigation.*

## Rules for transparency: redesigning the context

The police-accused interactions need to be similarly taped or video graphed as the case may be. This may seem simplistic and a minor issue of detail but as mentioned in *Introduction*, it is precisely these micro rules of interaction, and the consequential changes in the context, that are likely to bring about the outcomes desired, rather than grandiose plans or general and repeated instructions to the police about the need for transparency, objectivity and fairness. Once this is done, police may not be able to overwhelm the victim and the accused with their own interests—whether of the department (not recording an FIR to show reduced crime), or personal to the police officer (corruption). An ancillary benefit will be that the manipulative complainants who manage to get the FIRs registered in explicit or implicit collusion with the police may be exposed without inflicting much social damage.

The metro rail example given above highlights what Malcolm Gladwell calls 'power of the context' and the potential of small changes, such as removing graffiti, to bring about radical results such as orderly and peaceful travel in the New York metro; a small alteration in the working environment of a police station, as proposed, may bring about a transformational change in police behaviour.

## Justice for victims: from bystanders to stakeholders

We also need to consider the victim's interests during the stages of investigation and prosecution. In modern societies, the state takes responsibility for providing justice to victims by expending resources on the prosecution and incarceration of criminals. Sometimes, the victim or his/her family may have little interest in having the criminal punished and may like to forgive, with or without compensation. There is at present no way to do so, unless the police cooperate. This can lead to perverse consequences. If a criminal has gained Rs.1 lac from a particular crime in terms of utility but the victim has no stakes in the matter, the optimum strategy for the other two parties—policeman and criminal—is to share the gains as the victim is out of the picture. Jared Diamond, in a Chapter of his book, *The World Until Yesterday*—'*Compensation for the death of a child*', refers[8] to different systems of civil and criminal justice in traditional and modern societies and how the norms of criminal and civil justice in traditional societies differ from modern systems; the latter provide little scope for restorative justice or emotional closure for the victims and their families. He indicates how, in New Guinea, *Sori money* (meaning sorry money in *Tok Pisin*, the lingua France of New Guinea) or what may be crudely called compensation, is used to achieve satisfactory closure without the intervention of the police. In India, most of the cases, where victims may be happy with compensation, are now settled informally with the victim having to be declared a 'hostile witness' by the court. These rituals of prosecution and trial can result in a huge social waste in terms of transaction costs imposed not only on the offenders tried for minor crimes, but also on the State criminal justice systems. Victims need to be brought in as direct stakeholders in the judicial process by giving them a voice and a say in the court proceedings and its decisions.

## Default rule for compounding of offences

There is a need therefore to have a relook at the provisions for compounding of offences. While it is not possible for modern societies to revert to primitive solutions and, say, cut off the nose of the criminal to satisfy the accused, it should be possible to allow compounding of an offence where the victim is willing to accept economic/financial compensation, at least in the case of a large category of crimes which are not heinous—culpable homicide not amounting to murder for example, or serious injury. Needless to say, only the courts would have power to accept or reject the compromise; this would ensure that the compromise is completely voluntary and is not made under duress. There was news about a case where some Indians convicted of murder in the UAE paid blood money of over Rs. 70 crore and thus escaped the death sentence. The news was welcomed in India—the accused were Indians after all. On the other hand, these sensible solutions tend to be ignored at home. Courts may not consider such mediation options even for offences where compounding is permitted, unless the lawyer presses for it.

## Restitution and compounding of offences

The US law provides for plea bargaining, where victims have a voice, and even the Indian law allows compounding under Section 320 of the Criminal Procedure Code. Unfortunately financial compensation for the victim is not a part of this compounding process. And the long list of offences has no obvious logic; there is little point in excluding serious injury (Section 326 of IPC) where just a tooth may be damaged. *The option of compounding will 'take off' and become popular only when the victims can get compensated/paid under law.* Moreover, compounding needs to be treated as the 'default' option by Courts, not only for the offences listed but for many others; the court should proceed with a case only if the victim is not satisfied with restitution and compensation and is keen on retribution and revenge. *Changing the law by providing that the court should consider compounding as a default rather than a residual option would itself make a big difference.*

Steven Pinker[9] mentions that *proportionality* is a characteristic feature of modern societies. This has led over time to reduced incidence of violence, according to him, not only in terms of a drop in the number of war fatalities over time but also in the quantum of punishment inflicted on criminals. Human beings are not simply numbers. Jesse J. Prinz, while emphasising the influence of upbringing and culture on human nature, remarks that we need to be concerned with "human natures rather than human nature"[10]. All criminals are not alike. Psychopaths, as Pinker remarks[11], make upto 1-3% of male population, account for 20-30% of violent crime and commit half the serious crimes. In the case of most of the crimes against individuals, an *a priori* criterion for deciding on *proportionality* should be interest of the victim, as distinguished from that of the society or state; the latter should be invoked only in limited cases of treason or terrorism for example. *The onus of deciding on the appropriate mode of justice needs therefore to be shifted from the State and the courts to the victim, not only in cases which are compoundable at present but many more, except those considered directly harmful to the state or society.*

## Police-criminal games: cooperation or collusion?

Axelrod remarks[12] that, unlike citizen to citizen interactions where societies need to encourage cooperative behaviour, in case of public regulations relating to crime, the state should keep in view the possibility of collusion or a*social* cooperation developing among the violators and the enforcers. Axelrod shows that in the Iterated Prisoners' Dilemma situations where multiple computer games are played among the same players, as against the classic one-time Prisoners' Dilemma situation, parties tend to develop a cooperative frame. Rules need to be so designed as to discourage such collusion among criminals and the police. Here what Axelrod calls 'being nice'—the criminal and the police being nice to each other—is generally a paying strategy for the two parties. Collusion among the police and criminals is a likely outcome in these 'positive sum' games (with gains possible for both parties) as contrasted with 'zero sum' games (one party's gain is other party's loss) like chess. Interactions between the habitual criminals and the police are subject to the logic of iterated games where mutual cooperation rather than exploitation is the best strategy. Collusion is the likely outcome of repeated interactions between the police and habitual criminals, though this may not apply to first time offenders who are in a way 'strangers' for the police. Probably 24/7 CCTV coverage of all exchanges and events at the police station may provide an effective weapon to encourage socially productive cooperation and discourage collusion.

It would appear that a few simple and inexpensive changes in the working environment may make crime management much more effective:

(i) **Registration of FIRs:** Maintaining separate identity of the First Information Report (FIR) and FIR registration. This can be done through a system of mandatory *acknowledgement* of the report or information in case of complaints given personally and real time recording or videography of the same—telephone/police control room/anonymous source etc.

(ii) **Central Role of the Victim in Compounding of Offences:** Liberal provisions for compounding of offences under Section 320 of the CrPC, and making it the default rule for Courts. This needs to be supported by incorporating the institution of financial compensation for the victims.

(iii) 24 Hour videography/CCTV in the police stations.

# Endnotes

1  *Report of the Committee on Reforms of Criminal Justice System,* March 2003, www.mha.nic.in
2  Lotte Jr., John, 2007, *Freedomnomics: Why The Free Market Works And Other Half-Baked Theories Don't.* Regnery Publishing, US.
3  Wilson, James Q 1989/2000, *Bureaucracy; What Government Agencies Do and Why They Do It,* Basic Books.
4  Tripathy, J.K., 2008, Reaching Out to People, TRICHY Community Policing Experiment, (in) *Splendour in the Grass,* Department of Administrative Reforms and Public Grievances, Government of India, Penguin Books, India.
5  Ramalingam, Ben , 2013, *Aid on the Edge of Chaos,* Oxford University Press, New York.
6  Ariely, Dan, 2010/2011, *The upside of Irrationality: The Unexpected Benefits of Defying Logic at Work and at Home,* HarperCollins, London.
7  Wilson, James Q. and Kelling, George L., 1982, 'Broken Windows: The Police and Neighborhood Safety', *The Atlantic Monthly* (March): 29–83.
8  Diamond, Jared, 2012, *The World Until Yesterday,* Allen Lane/Penguin.
9  Pinker, Steven, 2011, *The Better Angles of Our Nature,* Penguin.
10  Jesse, J. Prinz, 2012, *Beyond Human Nature: How Culture and Experience Shape Our Lives;* Allen Lane/Penguin.
11  Pinker, 2011, Ibid.
12  Axelrod, Robert, 1984/Revised ed 2006, *The Evolution of Cooperation,* Basic Books.

# 7
## Bureaucracy
### Playing the Game of Honesty

I had analysed, in *Governance Unbound*, various facets of corruption and emphasised the need to orient and sensitise anti-corruption strategies to the specific context of corrupt exchanges and interactions—contracts may be collusive and involve 'grand corruption' whereas corruption in the delivery of basic services may be extractive but limited to small sums of 'speed money'. The focus here is on the laws and rules (e.g. *Prevention of Corruption Act*, Conduct Rules) designed to keep the bureaucrats honest and how these can be made more effective.

## Civil service pay and corruption

One reason which is usually believed to be responsible for a corrupt bureaucracy in the developing countries is low pay, but that may no longer be true at least in India, thanks to the recent Pay Commissions. In fact, for the lower and middle rungs of bureaucracy, and given the profile of national per capita and median income, average emoluments and perks of government officials would probably exceed those of the comparable categories in the private sector. Moreover, the top bureaucracy, which may not be as well fed as its counter parts in the corporate world, can hardly cite in its defence, as politicians tend to do, the compulsions of electoral politics for money making.

What seems to make a difference is not so much the cultural and social explanations but the structure of laws and rules which affect incentives and behaviour of bureaucrats. Singapore is one outstanding example of a change which is not primarily due to a revolution or high wages or culture, though wages have no doubt helped, but the institutions and rules designed for this purpose. In the case of India, basic laws such as the PCA (Prevention of Corruption Act) do matter but what may be more relevant are the rules in small print which operationalise the basic statutes and how these affect bureaucratic behaviour in actual situations of corrupt transactions.

## Prevention of Corruption Act: incentives for lavish consumption?

The PCA is the basic law for control of corruption and, with various amendments made from time to time, is generally comprehensive in scope. The provision of the PCA Act for punishment for the possession of assets disproportionate to income is especially innovative. This provision is unique in criminal law as no proof of intent is needed in cases where the fact of assets being disproportionate to the sources of income is established. Despite this innovative provision, the law does not seem to be serving its purpose due to one major lacuna; the lacuna is that expenditure, and the lavish life style and consumption it entails, is excluded from the definition of criminal conduct. This provision was introduced about 50 years back when there were not enough opportunities for consumption and the obvious and possibly the only option for parking illegal funds at least for most of the middle level bureaucrats was hoarding of assets—gold or real estate or even stuffing money under mattresses and in cupboards. Today free markets have spurred expensive consumption habits and the potential for consumption is practically limitless. Education of a ward in a foreign country even in an undergraduate course can cost over $50000 year; school education even in a private boarding school in India can cost a year's salary for a senior bureaucrat. It is also not very difficult to hide assets and bring them into use after retirement; some bureaucrats are known to indulge in a sudden flurry of buying expensive cars and houses just after retirement! It is, however, difficult to spend and consume without leaving a trail and salt away conspicuous consumption in Swiss bank accounts! We need therefore to consider not only the assets but also the life style, consumption and expenditure, of officials while deciding whether a bureaucrat should be indicted for corruption.

Consumption is much more visible than assets as the opaque land markets in India allow real estate to be a secret parking place apart from bank lockers and so on. A small change in the Act to include expenditure and consumption alongwith assets as ingredients of disproportionate assets may be a 'game changer' in providing appropriate (dis) incentives for officials. And it probably does not matter whether it is described as a 'nudge' or a 'kick'.

## Integrity codes and pledges

Barring this example where the main statute needs a review, we need to look into the rules of the game governing corrupt interactions which shape incentives and determine the outcome of such policies. Governments and the advocacy NGOs tend to focus on grand designs, tough penalties, generic integrity pledges, guidelines and codes of conduct but these mostly lie forgotten in the executive suites and conference halls and are rarely a factor in influencing choices. The reason is that these pledges and guidelines are not salient and immediately 'available' for recall in the actual situations which provide scope and temptation for corruption. Research has demonstrated the effectiveness of interventions which are nested in, and appropriate to, specific contexts and situations. In Uganda, information released to the newspapers by the Education Minister, regarding the grants given to different schools, made a difference in actual utilisation. In Indonesia, just the possibility of external audit led to a proper utilisation of road construction funds; social audit through local committees however did not make much difference.

## Contextual cues and 'nudges'

What seems to make a difference is immediate contextual cues, warning and nudges. In an experiment where consumers had to deposit money in a box for the coffee cups consumed, just a poster display of a pair of eyes (or even a coconut, put up as a representation thereof) staring at the customers made a difference in the total amount deposited by customers. A group 'primed' with the recall of the Ten Commandments acted much more honestly than the control group. Incentives provided by the rules need to be relevant to the specific situations involving behaviour, action and choice by the players and behaviour needs to be 'primed' by contextual rather than general cues and signals.

Public campaigns against cigarette smoking have had some success but a similar approach may not be very relevant in the case of corruption; in the former case, social marketing is effective as it is closely linked to the actual situations of temptation (e.g. display of pictures of the damaged lungs on cigarette packs). As however explained in the chapter on smoking, even this does not seem to work for habitual smokers. In Singapore and

Hongkong, advocacy campaign against corruption was directed mainly at the private business bureaucracies; corruption among the government employees was mainly addressed through the mechanism of negative incentives and aggressive enforcement by the Corrupt Practices Investigation Bureau (CPIB) in Singapore and Independent Commission Against Corruption (ICAC) in Hongkong. An appropriately designed screen saver on the desk tops and computers of officials—and similar posters at the front desks of the public agencies—will probably be much more effective than lectures and integrity codes!

## Myth of zero tolerance

Zero tolerance in the case of corruption is a myth and unlikely to work. We often hear affirmations that corruption, big or small, will not be tolerated in any form but such claims ignore certain behavioural dispositions of humans. As has been shown by Dan Ariely[1], the honesty monitor for most of the humans is active only in the case of major acts of corruption. Very few humans are sensitive to or bothered about their own or others' *small acts of dishonesty*—using the official car for shopping, using government stationery for private work and so on. On the other hand, a large number of corruption cases taken up by the anti-corruption bureaus happen to be about minor corrupt practices by the lowly employees. Governments could consider excluding such small acts of corruption and focus instead on the big fish and tackle 20% of (senior) employees who account for 80% of corruption. Anti corruption campaigns directed at the gazetted officers of a few 'wet' departments—police, taxation, revenue etc.—may pay huge dividends; they are more salient, well covered by the media and more likely to help build social norms among the bureaucrats.

## Creating Impact: the 80:20 rule

Prosecution of the small fry in fact can create a sense of unfairness (the feeling that big fish go scot free) among the employees. Employees' faith in the government's seriousness in tackling corruption is likely to be proportional to the frequency of high profile cases—these are more visible and have more impact. Small windows will continue to be broken and Wilson's theory of 'Broken Windows'[2]—take care of small violations and the bigger ones will disappear—is unlikely to work in the area of corruption.

We generally distinguish small acts of corruption (speed money or retail corruption) from grand or big ticket corruption. The ceiling on speed money is set by the likely transaction costs. Such small acts of corruption, where the supply-side incentive is simply minimising the transaction costs, are unlikely to provide adequate incentives for complainants or whistleblowers. Anti-corruption bureaus need therefore to concentrate on big ticket corruption rather than corrupt acts of the small fry most of whom may be only reducing the transaction costs imposed by the complicated and unimaginative rules. In fact, the responsibility for dealing with corruption at the lower levels of bureaucracy has better be left to the concerned department or agency. We are aware of the heuristics which bureaucracies follow—even a weak signal is sufficient for the bureaucracy to avidly shift responsibility to others. Many cases of small aberrations where departmental action may be more relevant are simply delegated upwards, to the anti corruption and vigilance bureaus!

## Rules in small print

Sometimes the operational rules themselves encourage gaming or escape strategies. One major example of a minor rule, incorporated in the IAS Conduct rules, is regarding the annual reporting of assets owned and acquired. On surface, these rules appear to be very well designed even though most of these are violated in practice. In North India, for example, the practice of reporting the acquisition of cars, TVs and other expensive stuff exceeding a specified monetary limit stands practically discontinued. More important, the rules leave major loopholes for officers who are required to report acquisition of property and file annual reports. One of these is an innocuous clarification [(Letter No. 5/4/74-AIS (III), dated 21$^{st}$ February, 1974), All India Services (Conduct) Rules, 1968]: *Properties acquired by the members of the family of the moS from out of their own funds need not be included in the property return of moS.* It is apparently an innocent clarification; why should a wife/ husband or son/daughter of an officer who has independent sources of income (called MoS in the rules—member of service) be expected to report assets in the MoS's returns? The problem is that the clarification depletes this rule and makes it meaningless. One can merrily buy property in the name of family members, *not report* the same by taking shelter under this rule and if case of a challenge much later, the authorities can only twiddle their thumbs and refer the matter of under or unreported income of the spouse to the income tax authorities! There have been cases of officers who purchased property in the name of parents and had the same gifted back to their children; and some clever ones acquired property in the name of parents and had their children formally adopted by the grandparents.

As indicated earlier, the concept of 'nudges' and mild incentives to encourage or discourage specific behaviour has become popular in the design of policy. The 'official' clarification regarding the asset reporting rule mentioned above is a perverse 'nudge' which is likely, on the other hand, to push bureaucrats towards non or under reporting of assets. Rules in small print continue to determine, in this as in many other areas of public governance, the fate of electoral promises and slogans.

## 'Honest' reporting of assets

Then there is the issue of reporting assets truthfully. Conduct Rules for officials in India contain admonitions for filing timely information and Returns about property; it is considered a serious misconduct. *There is however no disincentive and penalty for those who may be tempted to provide false or incorrect information which has in any case a low probability of coming to official notice, especially when the information is not placed in the public domain.* The Lokpal Act provisions appear to fare no better. *There is therefore little incentive for 'honest' reporting of assets let alone 'honest' acquisition thereof.*

It is not clear why corruption is endemic among the bureaucracy: is it something inherent in the nature of work or the power they exercise or the context, circumstances and incentives which tend to transform most of them from (the expected role of) 'robots', mechanically complying with rules[3], or of public spirited 'knights' to 'knaves'? Possibly one reason is the depersonalized nature of corruption in governance interactions (interactions between the official and the private entity), say, in contracts, purchases and sales, where the loser is not a person but an amorphous entity—the government. That may be one reason that such acts don't tend to being about the feeling of guilt and shame which is likely to be experienced when friends and 'in group' members are exploited. That may explain the ruthless exploitation of hapless citizens especially by agencies such as the police and the revenue officials.

Whatever the reasons, we need to move from ideological and idealistic advocacy, policy design and penalties, and factor in the behaviour of honest and corrupt actors while designing rules of the game. An unrealistic and generic approach, divorced and delinked from specific situations and context, may win votes but is unlikely to be helpful. Small may or may not be always beautiful but does matter. Basu has given a proposal for addressing the problem of 'harassment corruption'; this is to decriminalize the act of bribe-giving and to encourage the bribe-giver to be the whistleblower/witness[4]. This is not possible today as the law treats both the bribe-giver and the bribe-taker as culprits, ignoring the fact that most of corruption is in the nature of extortion[5]. I don't think this is a good idea and probably the problem of petty corruption has better be left to the departments rather than loading the anti corruption agencies. In the case of grand corruption, petty corruption is not an issue as most of these grand larcenies are collusive and this sort of 'invisible foot' strategy, which may be relevant for the PNDT Act (Chapter 2) would not be effective here. In any case, I have rarely heard of the CBI or any other agency ever prosecuting both parties; they need the bribe-giver as a witness or an approver.

The law needs to be amended to consider consumption alongwith assets for assessing whether expenses and assets are disproportionate to the sources of income. Property returns of high officials (including their family members) need to be in the public domain. And most important, a false declaration needs to be declared an act of misconduct. These somewhat mild changes in the statute and the rules may be more effective than awareness campaigns and integrity pledges.

## Endnotes

1 Ariely, Dan, 2010, *Predictably Irrational,* Harper Collins, UK.
2 Wilson, James Q. and Kelling, George L., 1982, 'Broken Windows: The Police and Neighborhood Safety', *The Atlantic Monthly* (March): 29–83.
3 This aspect has been elaborated in Basu, Kaushik, 2016, *An Economist in The Real World: The Art of Policymaking in India,* Penguin/Viking.
4 Basu, 2016, Ibid.
5 Jacoby, Neil H., Nehemkis Peter and Ells, Richard 1977 *Bribery and Extortion in World Business,* Macmillan Publishing, New York, explain this aspect of corruption.

# 8

# Dedicated Bureaucracy
## The Carrot or the Stick?

Indian bureaucracy does not enjoy a good image. While it is generally presumed to be lacking in the three vital Es necessary for good governance—ethics, efficiency and effectiveness—the picture is probably one-sided. There are many examples of deviation from this 'norm' and a bell curve would be a more accurate representation, may be with a much longer tail on the debit side. The issue examined here is the role that the policies and practices of rewarding the meritorious and weeding out the dead wood play in shaping the role, behaviour and incentives of the government officials. We need to keep in view that civil servants are also human and no doubt rational but they are also subject to cognitive and affective biases and limitations, and the common assumptions (black and white or 'knave' and 'knight'), which form the basis of the regulations governing them, may turn out to be rather simplistic.

## Fairness in giving rewards

One important issue is whether the rules and institutions of reward and punishment are perceived by the human employees as fair and objective; perception may matter more than rules or facts. And these subjective impressions and perceptions are to some extent themselves a function of cognitive biases. In matters involving the selection of a few to the inevitable exclusion of others, whether for performance pay or promotion or plum postings, it is difficult for the large majority of employees who are left out to be convinced of the government's objectivity and fairness. This may be partly due to the well known bias of 'over confidence,' illustrated by the well known finding that 90% of the car drivers believe they are above average! More employees than can possibly be selected may genuinely believe that they are brilliant or above average and therefore will be always convinced that the rewards, promotions and so on are biased, subjective and involve favouritism; this is a basic behavioural limitation we need to accept while addressing the issue of motivating them. One can ignore for the moment the added problem in India—the government's (or rather the proximate principals') capacity to be *really* impartial all the time, in the face of the well known political and personal whims and pressures. It may not therefore be realistic to expect the large majority of employees to have confidence in the fairness and impartiality of the government, despite formal assertions in the rules to this effect and even though the processes of selection and promotion may be fair and impartial most of the time. Various measures of assured career progression devised for employees who, though suitable, may not get promoted for lack of vacancies, are unlikely to help. People inevitably assess and evaluate themselves in comparison to others, especially those they consider their peers. Assured career progression schemes which provide for advancement of the officials unlucky enough not to be promoted (the number of higher positions being limited) label them as 'also-rans' and are unlikely to change their perceptions about selections being fair.

It may not be out of place to illustrate these problems by the institution of empanelment of the IAS officers for various posts in the Central Government (Joint Secretary/Additional Secretary/Secretary). The process of empanelment is taken up once a year. A committee consisting of three or four Secretaries headed by Cabinet Secretary is expected to evaluate the relative records (generally the last five years' ACRs) and select say 20 or 30 officers, out of the eligible bureaucrats, may be over 200, for the posts of Secretary (the number selected is obviously more at the lower level of Joint Secretary). The procedure is different from the common practice in the case of promotions for most of the senior posts in government, which is to consider five officers for one vacancy and so on; anybody who has been part of the process knows the difficulty of selecting only one officer from among the competing five and it is only natural, even assuming objectivity and impartiality on the part of a Selection Committee, that the results may be very different from common perception, especially given the variability and (lack of) validity and reliability of the ACRs under the present system. In any case, the seniors who are ignored are not likely to endorse the result for the reasons mentioned.

These problems are multiplied when the number of persons to be considered is large and a committee rather than an individual is required to consider and evaluate the relative records. Various experiments have shown that, whether in identifying tones of music or perfumes or flavour of teas, people find it difficult to discriminate beyond a limited range of options; this range is George Miller's 'magical number seven', which is the basis of the design of telephone numbers and vehicle registration. Human beings don't have the cognitive capacity to grasp or register characters or information beyond this number.

Making a choice is much more difficult due to 'option overload' and thus extraneous factors—first impressions or personal knowledge or, more likely, 'group-think'[1]—may take over; members may blindly endorse the choice made by an aggressive member or, more frequently, the boss!

The problem therefore seems to lie in the design of the institutions or rules of selection. It is impossible to make an objective selection, given the large number of options, especially as most of those eligible are placed in the top category of performers; their ACRs are 'outstanding'. We are not equipped to make a comparative assessment involving such huge numbers and, therefore, need quantitative and objective markers, algorithms and rules for selection as proposed elsewhere.

It is, therefore, unlikely that governments can win over the trust and faith of officials so long as they continue with the present institutional structures for rewards and promotions.

## Fairness in awarding punishment

It is, however, possible to address the pervasive perception, justified or not, of a lack of fairness in imposing punishments. One reason is that the grounds for punitive action are required by the rules to be much more concrete than in the case of promotions, postings and transfers etc. which are by nature based on a number of unquantifiable factors and involve making choices among a number of similarly placed competing employees. The rules for protecting employees against unfair punishment are much more precise and clear. Moreover the number of employees affected, unlike those affected by promotions and recognition, is relatively small and the penal processes do not require any comparative assessment of conduct. Except, therefore, for a few who may be prone to a persecution complex, self serving biases are not likely to create a general feeling of unfairness so far as the institutions of punishment are concerned.

## 'Trickle-down' of penalties and punishment

Rules for punishment or sticks can therefore be much more effective than carrots in providing incentives for performance and conduct but this is not what happens. It is rarely possible to dismiss an employee for various reasons, whatever the charge. This is true the world over. In the UK for example a committee comprising representatives of labour and management have to agree when some action is contemplated against a worker. What is surprising is that it is difficult in India to administer even minor penalties to the public sector employees. One reason is the centralisation of the disciplinary powers. There is little point for example in declaring that only the Head of the Department is competent to administer even a minor punishment, say for an entry level agricultural worker (*beldar*) working in a district. The competent authority for inflicting even a minor punishment may be five or six steps up in the hierarchy; these officers are not in a position to internalise or empathise with the mores, perspectives and information base of officials who are the immediate supervisors of the delinquent employees. The psychological distance means it is just another file; a detached response of 'It's Somebody Else's Problem' (ISEP) is quite common when a senior officer, many hierarchical rungs up and away, has to decide such cases. In Punjab, a very senior and well spoken officer, while admitting the appeal of an employee, even stayed the orders of dismissal passed by a Commissioner, orders which are effective from the date of issue!

The analogy of severe penalties including death penalty for heinous crimes which rarely act as deterrents will be appropriate. It is generally agreed that death penalty (whether it should continue is another issue) is hardly a deterrent for criminals; the main reason is that it is rarely administered in practice. This problem holds with much more force for dismissals and other government sanctions for the errant bureaucrats. Very few employees happen to be punished and the probability of punishment is negligible and hardly a deterrent for an average bureaucrat, especially when compounded with the problem of delinquent officials who are confident of escaping punishment. It is not very clear whether fruits of development trickle down to the poorest as some economists claim, but in the case of punishment of employees, it is definitely an invisible trickle down from the top.

And in the government set up, a number of other options to get out of the punishment trap are available. While posted as a Joint Secretary in the state government, I had to take up, somewhat reluctantly for the reasons mentioned, a departmental enquiry and on the basis of clear evidence of moral turpitude strongly recommended dismissal of the indicted officer; I happened to be posted back as Secretary in the same department after some years and found to my horror the very person coming for a courtesy call; on informal enquiry I found that even the file regarding the inquiry and my report was missing!

## Impact of the toxic institution of transfers

Governments, in the States and the Centre, therefore, are rarely able, whether in rewards or punishment, to give an image of fairness and impartiality. The institution of transfers makes matters worse. I am not aware of any country outside the South Asian region having this toxic institution which was perceptively described by a foreigner, Robert Wade, as a 'transfer industry' 30 years back[2]. The irony, and in fact the illegality involved in the appropriation, by the departmental ministers, of the powers of transfer even of the employees whose *appointing authority* may for example be the district head, has probably gone unnoticed. Transfers appear to have become a major and visible symbol of patronage and *have made the traditional rewards and punishments—promotions and penalties—irrelevant in the rational calculus of the government officials.*

## Rules and gaming strategies

Premier services such as the IAS whose members probably need more than monetary incentives for motivating them appear to be the most affected. It is rare for an IAS officer to be awarded even a minor punishment; in fact there may be more cases of dismissal than of minor punishment. It is not only impossible to comply with the complex, opaque and somewhat pointless provisions of the Punishment and Appeal Rules; it is even difficult to remember them well enough to apply in actual situations. I have yet to come across any serving officer who did not try to get out of the job of an Enquiry Officer precisely for this reason. No wonder the defending employees have a field day in the course of various appeals and revisions. One can only hope that bureaucrats will continue to perform their duties on the basis of what can only be described as *sui generis* motives!

## Is bureaucracy over-protected?

Given these administrative and behavioural constraints and the dim prospect of motivating employees through the present institutions, whether for reward or punishment, perhaps we need to redesign the rules. There has been a lot of discussion about employees being overprotected under the Indian Constitution. It is, however, not the constitutional protection which is the problem; *the constitutional protection*

*(Article 311) is probably no different from the protection to labour in the private sector provided under the Labour Laws.* The problem, on the other hand is about the elaborate and over protective rules. The IAS Punishment and Appeal Rules run into fifty pages and have complicated rules which seek an impossible compromise between adequate opportunity for the defence at *each and every stage* of the proceedings and the need to administer speedy decisions. Some of the clauses—time for filing a reply, contents of the charge sheet and the level of proof required—probably match, if not exceed, the protection provided to the accused under the provisions of the CrPC and the Indian Evidence Act.

## More loyal than the King!

Governments and their agencies seem to be fond of scoring own goals by designing operational rules of the game which are orthogonal to the stated objectives and encourage perverse responses. And probably the courts cannot be blamed; they only want the government to follow its own rules strictly which, as explained above, is an almost impossible task. The problem is neither the constitution nor the courts but the governments' own ham-handedness in the drafting of rules which appear to be more loyal to the bureaucrats than the king, the state.

Unfortunately, we humans are designed to respond to broad narratives and macro aspects of the basic policy and laws; these are more visible and, as behavioural economists say, 'available'; we tend to neglect the design of rules in small print which may be more consequential in determining outcomes. Policy makers need to attend more to these minor and mundane aspects of governance, rather than grand designs and plans for rewards and punishments—performance pay, zero tolerance of corruption and so on. It may be too much to expect any major change in the institution of transfers. It is a public good for which individuals and organizations are not likely to band together to bring about a change. The concentrated and small group interests—in this case of individual employees or their benefactors, are, as has been shown[3] likely to prevail. But surely the institutions of promotion and punishment can be redesigned to be better aligned to the employee motivations, incentives and behaviour.

## Endnotes

1 Gladwell, Malcolm, 2000/2001, *The Tipping Point*, Abacus/Little Brown, London, p. 175.
2 Wade, Robert 1985, The Market for Public Office; *World Development*, Volume 13, No. 4.
3 Mancur, Olson 1965, *The Logic of Collective Action*, Harvard University Press, Cambridge MA.

# 9
# Performance Pay for the Bureaucracy

Government of India (GoI) has been considering the issue of performance linked pay for the bureaucracy. Successive Pay Commissions have also recommended this practice. It does not, however, appear to be a feasible proposition, especially when we have not been able to settle even the basic structure of salaries of the government employees—moving from a 'master scale' to 'grade pay' to what the latest Pay Commission describes as a 'matrix' pay structure.

## Practice in the Corporate Sector

In the first place, barring symbolic schemes, there is little possibility of the emoluments of bureaucrats being fully or substantially linked to performance. Even the private sector has not found it possible to link more than a fraction of the fixed monthly and annual wages to performance. In fact what is more common is a topping up of fixed salaries with bonuses and other incentives. There are enough horror stories about the top executives of some companies cornering fat bonuses, even when the institutions were on the verge of closure or bankruptcy—an obvious case of personally pleasant consequences of 'moral hazard.' And the investment and share trading firms have rarely instituted pay cuts even when the traders caused massive losses. A major feature of gifts and bonuses in the private sector is that these primarily cover only the middle and top management levels. Such 'deferential' treatment of executives, as distinguished from workers, defined as labour in India, is rarely possible within the government set up. Even for deciding on the emoluments for different ranks and grades of officials, the Pay Commissions used to follow the rule that the wage differential (maximum: minimum) should not exceed 10:1. This practice, however, has been more or less abandoned by the last two Pay Commissions; they now refer to these differentials in terms of the median wage (wages after say 15-20 years of entry) enjoyed by the highest and the lowest level workers, which to me is a patent instance of obfuscation. In any case, it is unlikely that in India pay structures for the middle and top ranks of the government officials and of course the Ministers, will match those in the corporate world; it may therefore be difficult to devise satisfactory models of performance pay for the top levels who earn only what one may call survival wages.

## Bureaucratic cadres, classes and norms

In fact, it may be difficult to link even a part of the wages in the government departments and agencies to performance. Officials belonging to different professions and specialities rarely identify themselves with a particular department. Engineers—whether in irrigation or power or roads departments—expect similar treatment across various departments. The administrative staff (assistants, clerks and so on) who work in different sectors and departments but are recruited mostly through a common selection system, and have similar qualifications, have their own professional identity. It is, therefore, difficult to start with a limited pilot or experiment for an appropriate design of performance pay or to restrict the practice to a few agencies.

Further, even though some of the outputs and outcomes of performance of a particular organisation may be measurable, the disparate cadres of administrative, technical and professional staff, whose relative contribution would naturally vary even within the same organisation, would expect identical treatment. The accountant in a college or a clerk in a school would not be left out, in case incentives are provided for the teachers. In the thermal power plants, in a power utility I headed, every cadre has to be a part of the incentive scheme irrespective of its contribution. The only concession implicitly agreed in such cases is to vary the proportion of the bonus—engineers get more than helpers and the administrative staff. Then there is the problem of perverse incentives such as reluctance to back down power generation when asked by the grid managers. There is little possibility, therefore, of even a pilot being introduced to test the validity of performance pay except for the highly specialised and what I call 'exo' agencies such as Space and Atomic Energy.

## Assessment of performance

Most of the government agencies perform activities whose outcomes and even outputs may be difficult to assess. James Q Wilson[1] has provided a classification of the government agencies in the USA, based upon the criteria of quantification and measurability of their activities and outcomes. If one goes by these criteria, only a few government units in India, whose activities as well as outcomes are quantitative and measurable, would qualify.

Then there is the fundamental problem of developing a reliable data base for a proper assessment of the relative performance of individuals, ignoring for the moment the problem of judging an agency's performance, in view of the difficulties indicated. So long as we continue with the practice of frequent transfers, with job tenures rarely coterminous with whatever time parameters may be used for the assessment of performance (say the financial year), linking even a part of the pay to performance may not be practicable in the Indian context, at least so far as the state governments are concerned, where the institution of transfers is deeply entrenched and, as in the case of Punjab, average tenure of most of the police officers may be even less than a year.

## Over-confidence bias and perception of fairness

The biggest hurdle may be the employee psyche. As psychologists have shown, most of us consider ourselves to be above average or brilliant and suffer from the bias of over confidence. The misconception is easier to nurse when the assessment of performance itself is not a simple process. An outsider's or even a superiors' judgement (even assuming, it is objective which may not always be the case) may create resentment instead of encouraging competition for excellence. Factors which matter for a general perception of fairness in the process of selection for performance pay may have nothing to do with the employee's own worth. In a famous study[2], capuchin monkeys were paired up and trained to surrender a token in order to receive a reward of cucumber slices. The subject monkey resented the discrimination when it saw another monkey being given a more desirable reward, grapes; it refused the humble reward of cucumber slices! Probably the deprived monkey rarely considers the possibility that the reward of the other capuchin is well deserved! Human beings have much more developed cognitive and self critical capabilities than monkeys but given the problems of measurement, frequent transfers, personal preferences and the biases mentioned above, even they may be unable to accept differential treatment, even where objectively justified.

Then there is the problem of gaming and manipulation of rules to gain personal advantage, which is likely to emerge close on the heels of a policy of performance pay and bonuses. The institution of the ACRs (Annual Confidential Reports) is an example. Anybody who has been a part of the Indian bureaucracy is aware of various strategies employed to gather outstanding ACRs. My batch mate in the Indian Administrative Service (IAS), M.K. Kaw, has given enough examples in his book *Bureaucrazy*. The sum of resentment, cynicism and criticism is likely therefore to far exceed that of satisfaction, happiness and motivation of the limited few who get the performance bonus. The social cost of such a measure therefore will far exceed the gains to a few. The amount of bonus is likely to translate into manifold social losses for those deprived, even though the process may be fair.

## Performance pay as entitlement

The idea of performance pay is no doubt attractive but it is unlikely to be politically saleable, administratively feasible or acceptable to the different categories of employees who may be excluded from the scheme or from its benefits. Such institutions are only likely to end up being viewed as *entitlements*. The complicated matrix of the bureaucratic - political hierarchy involved in making a judgement about individual merit, unlike the simpler and leaner control structures in the private sector, makes such choices difficult, controversial and so best avoided. Even in the USA, as James Q. Wilson referred above shows, the policy of linking a part (20%) of the pay to performance for the Senior Executive Service in the US has not been a success; in fact as he mentions, the *available budget for performance bonus was mostly distributed evenly over a large number of employees to minimise resentment.*

I spent some years working for a state government in the North-East of India. It was quite common there for the government employees to be described in this pithy manner: *offishe jai, maina pai, kaaj korte overtime chai* (I get paid for going to office and need overtime if I have to work). Of course, it is a false stereotype of the government employees in general or those of a particular region. The general point is that governments will do well just to ensure that the routine government work and activities are carried out efficiently, before thinking of monetary incentives for encouraging exceptional performance.

There is one other aspect, that of 'moral hazard'. None of the officials or ministers awarding bonuses on a liberal scale under such a scheme would have any 'skin in the game'; unlike the Board of Directors of a company, they don't have profits or survival at stake and the survival problem is likely to be transferred from the individual agency doling out bonuses to the nation and its economy, and may end up as the last straw on the camel's back, budget deficit! Given therefore the context, norms and incentives structures, selective bonuses and rewards for officials are unlikely to work in India.

## Endnotes

1  Wilson, James Q., 1989/2000, *Bureaucracy; What Government Agencies Do and Why They Do It*, Basic Books.
2  Brosnan, Sarah F. and de Wall, Frans B.M., Monkey Reject Unequal Pay: Nature, 425, p. 297-299, 18 September 2003.

# 10

## Indian Bureaucracy
### Thinking Outside the Box

The Indian Government is taking a number of steps to revive and inject dynamism into the economy. Apart from economic initiatives, the paradigm of governance is also being dusted off the shelf and sought to be internalised into the routines of governmental functioning. One of the areas being discussed in regard to bureaucrats, the implementers of policy and programs, is encouraging them to be innovative. Given the governance structure in India where the Secretariat dominates the quality of decision making and outcomes, it may also be appropriate to redesign the operational rules of the Secretariat; the present focus is only on the Executive wings—the line departments and bureaus. The Secretariat should also be able to encourage and promote innovation not only in the executive agencies but also in its own ranks.

## Culture of conformity

Encouraging and nurturing innovation among bureaucrats is rather problematic and the current institutions are in fact designed to suppress it, whatever its origin—desk or field. Most of the private organisations are, or at least were in the past, single purpose and cohesive units dominated by specific professions, branded products or in the case of the

NGO's, a specific mission or charter. In contrast, most of the government departments are rarely organised around any 'core competency'. Political and social constraints make it practically impossible and, in the process of having to conform to these constraints rather than concrete goals, the safe bet for officials is the shelter provided by routines and the Standard Operating Procedures (SOPs). The conformist culture is ably supported by the formal rules of conduct and propriety, hierarchical relationships and top down systems.

The Central Secretariat Manual of the Government of India had a specific provision earlier which was meant to discourage the expression of dissenting opinion in the course of official noting by the long hierarchy of officials— Assistant/SO/US/DS/JS/AS/Secretary. Any difference of opinion was expected to be resolved first in meetings/ discussions with the seniors. The hierarchical order and the prevailing culture, however, had raised the innocuous provision, which was originally meant only to prevent unproductive dissent, to a pedestal. In the 1970's one of my batch mates working as an Under Secretary in a ministry, notorious for the practice of pasting or removing the 'inconvenient' notes of juniors, confronted his Joint Secretary who consoled him by taking out of the side cupboard a sheaf of his own notes removed from various files by *his* seniors!

With the passage of time such obviously illogical rules have been modified but only on surface. Latest provisions of the Secretariat Manual, downloaded from the internet, indicate that this provision is no longer there but the culture continues. During my stint with a private sector outfit after retirement, I was told by the dealing officials of a powerful ministry, which had to decide on a request made by the organisation I was working for, that *they would put up the file only if requisitioned by the seniors*. We had to request the

PMO to intervene and this was necessary even to deal with the FR (fresh receipt), the request made by us; the desk officers did not even have liberty to put up the case files, let alone give their opinion! Moreover, a number of tricks are available to the seniors in the hierarchy to suppress dissent. I have, however yet to see any senior being chided, let alone punished, for this. The dominant culture is still a lack of tolerance for a different view point, especially if expressed by a junior. Within the government agencies, rank equals wisdom.

## Cognitive dissonance: the end game

Government rules and instructions do provide protection to officers refusing to carry out illegal orders but in the case of any difference of opinion (say on a particular investment or a purchase decision), the only right one has is that of a second referral. The consequences for dissent are similar in all situations, whether an honest difference of opinion or a conflict between public interest and the private motives of some of the officials: an assignment in the backwaters of the agency, or reversion to the state cadre. One need not be a *homo economicus* or a 'rational agent' to make the choice; even a *Homo sapiens* with all her irrationalities and biases, understands the threat this ritualistic right to refer back can create to her survival. The result is compliance with 'top down' thinking and opinion all around. A few of those who cannot adjust to this 'cognitive dissonance' between the reality and their beliefs have chosen to resign. Many others have rationalised and reconciled by adjusting their beliefs and conduct to reality.

## 'Wisdom of the Crowd' of bureaucrats

The government needs to set down clear rules which lift the informal embargo on dissent and encourage expression of honest opinion. It may take time for the new culture to sink in but it is worth working for. It is the younger cadres and age groups who are biologically equipped to innovate, not the officers about to board the retirees' train to senescence. Remarkable results have been achieved by many young officers who happen to be posted in autonomous boards, executive agencies and districts where they are not so stifled by the hierarchies and have clear tasks, in Surat, Ahmednagar, Tiruchy and many others. Similar innovations are possible even in the government secretariats, if the culture of wooden compliance and 'group think'[1] can be changed. The desk jobs need creativity and innovation as much, if not more than, field assignments.

James Surowiecky in *The Wisdom of Crowds*[2] (2004) has pointed out some pre-requisites for the 'crowd' to be collectively wise. One of these is that the individuals need to exercise independent opinion and must not indulge in 'group think'[3]. Unless rules encourage dissent in ideas and opinion, the decisional outcomes of the elaborate hierarchy, which despite many other problems it can give rise to, has been created precisely for providing diverse inputs, will only result in top down decision making.

## Endnotes

1 Janis, Irving, 1983, *Group Think*, revised 2nd ed. Houghton Mifflin, Boston.
2 Surowiecki, James, 2004/2005, *The Wisdom of Crowds: Why the Many Are Smarter Than the Few and How Collective Wisdom Shapes Business, Economics, Societies and Nations*, Abacus, Little Brown, UK.
3 Janis, Irving, 1983, Ibid.

# 11

## Labour Laws
### The Devil's in the Detail

In a Chapter, *Death by Lime Register* (Lime Register refers to the register to be maintained under the Factories Act for whitewashing operations), Mihir Sharma has documented governance failure of the labour laws[1]. The consequence of these silly regulations, as he notes, is that businesses with less than 10 workers employ over 90% of India's workers; if you employ or show more workers, you are subject to the *'Nice, Kindly Government Inspector'* —the ironical title of one of the sections of his book.

Government of India is very much aware of these problems and has come out with a basket of reforms in the labour laws. Some of these aim at improving the image of India in respect of the ease of doing business; the current ranking of India is a shame (out of 189 countries, India ranks 130). Some other measures seek to improve labour welfare. In the first category we have proposals such as (a) raising the threshold of the number of workers under The Factories Act from 10 (with power) and 20 (without power) to 20 and 40 respectively; (b) preventing misuse by the inspecting officials by shifting from selective and ad hoc inspections to random inspection systems and immediate uploading of inspection reports; (c) liberalising overtime restrictions. The second group covers measures such as a unique account number for each worker to be used across different welfare and security regulations—CPF (Contributory Provident Fund), ESI (Employees State Insurance) etc. and more canteens, lunchrooms and protective equipment for labour. There is another set of rules aimed at the facilitation of processes and modernisation of laws and rules such as electronic Returns, simplification of forms and so on which would make life easy both for owner and labour. The question is whether these changes will address the problem of the 'regulatory cholesterol' (though the term now seems to be a misnomer in the light of the latest research which shows that cholesterol is not the problem it was earlier thought to be) and provide adequate vascular space to improve the sclerotic labour markets.

Democratic governments have generally little choice in matters of macro policy and regulatory design; these are mostly determined by ideology. Only the best and popular brands will do. The Minimum wage law, for example, has to be there, despite what most of the economists may say about its adverse impact on employment, especially new entrants and untrained workers. Some of the changes mentioned above are also in the process of being jettisoned due to pressure from various lobbies. While the broad regulatory structures are, therefore, likely to continue, that need not prevent the government from attending to the damage caused by the rules in small print, such as the lime register, which operationalise the basic laws and do not need any statutory amendments. There are a number of areas where attention to these rules of the game may be helpful both for labour and management, lead to more efficient and productive social outcomes and substantially improve the ease of starting and doing business in India.

## Licence—permit raj goes underground

It is generally claimed that licencing is not necessary for most of the manufactured goods; the claim is based on the abolition of the Industrial Development and Regulation Act. The provision for compulsory licencing under the Factories Act 1948, however, continues. Section 6 of the Factories Act, which prescribed registration and licencing, was actually only an *enabling* provision meant to be used restrictively "for any class or description of factories" which needed to be licenced and could be specified in the rules. The rules in most of the states, however, mandate universal licencing and cover practically all the factories under the Act; thus a factory for the manufacture of drugs which is regulated by an elaborate and somewhat complex Drugs Control Act needs a separate licence under the Factories Act. This licence raj under the Factories Act continues to this day not due to a parliamentary law but a set of rules under the Factories Act which operate beneath the radar of the policy makers. And this practice of redundant licencing continues, despite product and process specific laws on practically every possible activity which needs some regulation—sugar, cosmetics, drugs, food and so on. In fact, despite the anti-pollution laws, one still needs a clearance for hazardous substances under the Factories Act. There is little point in persisting with universal licencing under the generic provision made in the 1950's. This process alone means a delay of 2 to 3 months only to complete paper work and obtain permissions and clearances, even though, mercifully, as my investigations indicate, the staff may not expect much by way of speed money. Would it not be better if the rules could simply provide for compulsory registration, based on self-declared information about the factory, instead of continuing with the ritual of scrutiny of plans and physical inspection of projects which may be beyond the competence of inspecting staff, and in any case serves little purpose?

## Forms, registers and returns: wasteful rituals

The other issue is of the large number of Forms, Registers and Returns prescribed under the rules made under various Labour Laws. I got a list of various forms and returns compiled by an industrialist in Punjab which indicated that a total of 116 forms are required to be filed by a manufacturing unit, apart from a large number of periodical Returns. And then of course, there is the list of various Registers described by Mihir Sharma in his inimitable style, varying from muster roll, overtime, health, to humidity and of course the Lime Register. A new law (Exemption from Furnishing Returns and Maintaining Registers by Certain Establishments Act, 1988) had apparently simplified this process for small establishments but a perusal of the schedule of this Act indicates that this is not the case. Form B of the Schedule, register of wages, and Form C, muster roll, require too much detail most of which is prima facie pointless. Most of the establishments have in any case to maintain accounts including wage details in the standard accounting formats; they also need to get the accounts and balance sheets audited for income tax and VAT purposes. Further, these forms are not of much use in detecting violations and in the case of a complaint in any case, an enquiry is needed to establish facts. The Returns which are needed primarily for compiling data and statistics can thus be greatly simplified for that limited purpose. Further, it is not clear why, whatever the simplified formats, all the establishments—big or small—should not be covered under the law. One is mystified as to why the Labour department cannot rely on the commercially accepted accounting formats as the Tax departments do, instead of requiring factories to provide them repetitive information in slightly different formats. One can imagine the chaos if the Tax Department were to devise its own accounting formats!

In fact, the 1998 Law had almost 'nil' impact. In Punjab, as my enquiries show, not a single industrial unit has opted for it. It is generally assumed that industrial units do file Returns and do incur substantial harassment and transaction costs which the government can help eliminate through simplification, but the reality is different. Employers have already found a simple solution, not to file Returns. Penalties are negligible and in the face of universal non compliance, the probability of action low. In Punjab less than 5% of the employers file these Returns and the all India situation is unlikely to be much better. Probably the Labour Ministry do not even have the data. So what is the point of simplifying Returns which the industry is not bothered about, especially when the simplified Returns are not really that simple?

## Do we need these 'Declarations of Innocence'?

The Indian government continues to put its faith in the sanctity of forms and registers; there is little appreciation of the huge transaction costs imposed on the industry in maintaining duplicative muster and payrolls of labour when the required information is already available in the routine accounting systems. At the most the owners could be instructed to mention the unique number of each employee in various registers—muster roll/pay etc. and to maintain vital additional data—for example overtime—by adding a field in the digital accounting systems.

Further, even the limited numbers of Returns submitted by a few factories are simply filed away by the department. A similar fate may await the electronic Returns sought to be introduced now. In fact the Returns are not designed to provide the data and information which may help the labour departments in developing a proper data base at the state level; the only use of the Returns and forms is for selective nitpicking by officials, 'kindly inspectors' or corrupt officers. We also know that a large percentage of labour in the organised sector is 'shadow' labour, whatever the reasons—complex rules about minimum wages, competition and so on. The Returns are therefore likely to reflect only half truths. *These Returns are just 'declarations of innocence' and unlikely to reflect facts and reality.*

*We need to abandon the worthless institution of numerous records, Registers, and Forms and Returns, except for minimal governance—to get the relevant data, statistics and information the government needs, rather than an indicator of compliance or otherwise of the labour laws.*

## Law on minimum wages: The devil in the detail

Minimum Wages is another area where it is the rules in small print which create more distortions than the basic law. The annual notification of the Punjab Labour department on minimum wages covers four categories—unskilled, semi skilled, skilled and highly skilled and not only fixes minimum wages for each category but also defines over 100 designations included in one or the other category. *The notifications even specify the pay increase to be given when an employee moves, say, from unskilled to skilled category,* a sort of assured career progression scheme for the private sector labour! I have documented this absurdity in *Governance Unbound. The result is a spate of litigations caused more by these annual notifications than by the Minimum Wages Law itself.* Surely the problem of a race to the rock bottom of wages— surplus labour completing for limited employment—can be adequately addressed by enforcing minimum wages at the lowest level of entry—unskilled labour; competition for the higher level skills will probably find the equilibrium for the better qualified categories.

## Role of the labour bureaucracy: enforcement or mediation?

Another issue is that of the mode of enforcement—should government officials enforce the law or leave it to the aggrieved parties? Inspections are unlikely to provide information on the state of compliance due to problems, primarily of (lack of) information, and secondarily of incentives. Some facilities—canteens, lunchrooms—are now proposed to be extended to smaller size factories, presumably in aid of labour welfare. These facilities cost money and such sophisticated welfare measures may only end up providing convenient handles for the labour inspectors to extract money; the owner may still be better off. A modicum of attention to these aberrations of regulatory governance in the case of labour laws would make things easier not only for the corporates but also for labour and lead to more harmonious labour relations. In the US, 90% of cases of minimum wage violations are initiated on the basis of complaints from aggrieved labour; in India the position appears to be just the reverse, as my interaction with the district labour offices in Punjab indicated. The Labour Department needs to encourage workers and whistleblowers and should itself act only as a dispute settlement and mediation rather than enforcement agency.

It would be obvious that what needs to change is not the statute, but the operational rules intended to implement the basic laws, rules which seem to be fulfilling the agenda not of the policy makers but the labour inspectors. Why not leave it to the aggrieved party—labour and their unions—to find the optimum trade-off, or if that fails, complain and protest rather than multiply social costs—cost of maintenance of records and registers (owner), cost of ensuring compliance (government)—without any benefit to labour.

The economist Ronald Coase has demonstrated the advantage of this approach (*The Problem of Social Cost*). If labour is happy and compensated in some alternative fashion—for the lack of a canteen or a lunchroom or for extra hours beyond overtime limits—why should the government bother? And of course if the union or an individual is not satisfied, inspectors are always available for enquiry and inspection and can initiate penal and other actions. In any case, a number of gaming strategies are available to the owners—call a white collar worker an Executive or a blue collar supervisor as Assistant manager and he/she is out of the jurisdiction of labour laws!

Most of the business and even labour friendly measures can be initiated simply by an amendment of the rules:

**Discontinue licencing of factories:** Rules under the Factories Act need to provide only for registration based on self-declared information, in place of prior approval and licencing by the department.

**Discontinue (most of) the Forms, Registers and Returns:** Accept standard accounting formats used by Factories for salary, wages and other labour related matters. Discontinue various Registers and Returns (except for the vulnerable labour groups—child labour etc.).

Prescribe simple registers and abstract annual Returns purely for the purpose of collecting information and data and not for wasteful attempts to gather documentary evidence of misuse or violation of the law.

**Minimum Wages Law:** Simplify annual notifications fixing minimum wages: Specify only the minimum, entry-point wages for unskilled labour and leave it to market to find wage equilibrium for the rest.

**Encourage Self Enforcement/Bilateral Settlement:** Rely on workers and whistle blowers to signal violations and malpractices. Conduct inspections only in the case of complaints (except for laws regarding vulnerable groups).

## Endnotes

1 Sharma, Mihir, *Restart: The Last Chance for the Indian Economy 2015*, Random House, India.

# 12

## Public Services
### Moral Hazard of Self Certification

Most of the basic public services are "contingent, need based documentation services and are merely the enablers and gateways for social and economic opportunities (identity card, passport, domicile certificate, ration card, the UID). They have no direct relationship to any functional activity and are, if one may use the term, fungible like money"[1]. A residence or a caste certificate may be used for different purposes—a phone connection, employment, admission in a college. Some of the citizens may need and/or use them, others never or rarely. These services cover issues of identity and eligibility (Caste/Residence Certificate) and entitlement for various government programmes and schemes (old age pension and other similar social welfare measures). Then there are the functional and client oriented services such as licences, permissions and approvals for individuals (new construction, driving licence) and business entities (licencing, prior registration of factories) etc. which are covered in Chapter 13.

### Verification processes

Citizens and businesses who wish to avail of these services are required to fill up forms and provide personal, professional and business information. The standard procedure in such cases, till recently was: (a) an affidavit about identity and eligibility, (b) third party endorsement or confirmation of the claim, mostly by officials—elected or otherwise. In the case of some of the relatively more prized services—scheduled caste certificate/income certificate - an enquiry about the *bona fides* is conducted usually by the ubiquitous revenue official. This, unsurprisingly, consists typically of statements by a couple of 'respectable' residents (Lambardar, Panchayat members) endorsing the affidavit or the self certification by the beneficiary or the applicant, which is then duly certified by the revenue official.

## Affidavit vs self declaration

Delivery of these basic services can be and is being substantially improved by some simple administrative measures. One of these concerns the mandatory requirement of affidavit. An affidavit is an affirmation sworn before a notary and can be easily substituted by a cost effective and simple self declaration. That can save substantial transaction costs—typically about Rs. 300–500 for an affidavit, as estimated in the case of Punjab. Based on the extrapolation of the Punjab data, I had estimated[2] the annual volume of affidavits in India to be 30 crores annually—about one per household—which means that approximately Rs. 10,000–15,000 crore were being spent on this pointless exercise—purchasing stamp papers, typing the affidavits and getting them attested from a notary or a government official. The practice has now been discontinued and a simple self declaration is considered sufficient for this purpose.

## Self declaration or self certification?

That itself however is not adequate. The second step is accepting that self declaration; there is little point in eliminating affidavits if self declarations still need third party endorsement by public officials. For most of the basic services, there is little incentive in obtaining a false certificate as it is available for the asking if one is eligible. Moreover, these basic services have low utility and little scarcity value; anybody can have a ration card or a residence certificate; every person from a Scheduled Tribe is eligible for a scholarship. Bogus documentation in support of eligibility may open up some opportunities for a few, but is rarely a sufficient condition for entitlement. For example, while there is competition for employment against the quota reserved for the STs/SCs, the number of applicants is huge and a certificate is far from being a sufficient condition for employment. Moreover, the risk of misuse is minimal; competition for the benefits ensures that the misuse does not go unnoticed and the consequences then can be severe. There is, therefore, little advantage in setting up various filters and gatekeepers to check entitlements especially in the case of most of the basic services where an overwhelming majority are likely to make truthful declarations. Further, for the miniscule minority for whom some document or certificate may be terribly important (an emigrant needing a birth certificate for getting the citizenship of a foreign country), the check lists and endorsements can be easily negotiated and circumvented; it is all a matter of incentives.

The risk of misuse is thus best addressed by punitive measures taken *post facto*. There is little logic in loading the vast majority of compliant citizens, who have little reason or incentive to tell a lie, with huge transaction costs just to prevent a small minority from misusing the process, which in any case it is rarely possible to ensure. Moreover, the evidence of misdemeanour is always and readily available in a candidate's own false declaration and that is itself a big deterrent. Thus the institution of self certification which has been advocated[3] by academics and others, and can make life easy for all concerned, will only flow from a $360^0$ self declaration.

## Informational cascade

It also appears pointless, as I had elaborated in *Governance Unbound*, to employ resources of manpower and time for verification of facts and information, such as income, which are fully known only to the applicant. The only result of the verification processes therefore is an 'informational cascade': the applicant states something; the public official (especially if holding an elective position) has no other option but to believe it, and the government bureaucrat has to endorse it.

## Transaction costs

Governance exchanges in the case of basic services are by nature market transactions; the only difference is that these transaction costs matter much more than prices or the fees payable, which are mostly negligible and consequently the corruption or 'shadow' transaction costs per unit are also not very material. The potential for corruption would be further reduced with the introduction of online application and delivery systems, as in the case of passports. For these basic services which are contingent and involve one-off governance interactions, therefore, a market rather than a behavioural frame appears to be more suitable. *The focus should be on eliminating transaction costs by adopting self certification as the default rule for most of these services.*

## A nudge for truthful self declaration

As indicated above, administrative reforms which reduce transaction costs and provide simple default rules for officials would be adequate for most of these services but a behaviourally informed approach may be helpful in two areas of interaction: honest and truthful self reporting of personal information and simplifying the forms.

Governments try to ensure truthful declarations by the force of threats but as Halpern[4] observes "Even when such systems have been built, it often feels as if they result in quite a lot of hassle for the honest, while still remaining far from foolproof at catching the cheats". Moreover elaborate checks, verifications and threats of punishment for wrong statements may not achieve the objective of eliciting truth and honesty, and instead reinforce the wrong social norm: that most people are not to be trusted and do cheat[5]. It is therefore not only wasteful but downright dangerous to persist with rules providing for elaborate verification and scrutiny. Dan Ariely, the author of *Predictably Irrational* mentions the experiments he and his colleagues conducted which showed that the timing of the moral reminders matters; simply shifting the declaration to the top of the tax form in the USA could lead to more honest and truthful statements about taxes[6]. It is a different matter that they failed to persuade the IRS authorities in the US to make the change, an illustration of the power of inertia and status quo bias! Designing the forms to place the self declaration at the top of the form or application for a service, to be signed *before* one is asked to fill in the information, could make citizens significantly more honest and truthful.

## Simplification of forms

The tendency of the bureaucrats is to ask for as much information as they can think of, whether or not it has any relevance. While they may be very much aware of the time constraints for themselves—one hears constant complaints about work overload in government offices—they are happy to build such redundancies for the public! Governments need to provide information about checklists and procedures in a simple and understandable manner and simplify forms and applications. As Sunstein observes[7], these services are sometimes not availed of due to the complex processes prescribed under the regulations and simplification will enable more people to access the services and understand and make use of them. Sunstein gives the example of the simplification of applications forms for the student loans undertaken by the US Federal Government[8]. Simple changes such as pre-population of forms (entering particulars on the basis of the data available with the authorities already) led to a significant increase not only in the number of applicants and availment of loans but also of admissions. The process of simplification has to be done in house, keeping in view the objectives and nature of specific services, risk or misuse potential, and so on. Very few academics would have the dedication and clout of Sunstein who pioneered such processes as head of the OIRA in the USA, and it is unlikely therefore that this will happen even though very desirable and necessary.

It would appear that apart from creating a default rule for officials for accepting citizen affirmations at face value, governments can create a feeling of scarcity and competition to encourage self-correcting mechanisms (e.g. complaints by others who may be outcompeted by cheats). Affidavits or declarations also need to be redesigned by shifting the signed affirmations to the top of the forms and applications.

# Endnotes

1 Gupta, R.N., 2015, *Governance Unbound: Public Services, Players and Rules of the Game*, Aakar Books, Delhi.
2 Gupta, 2015, Ibid.
3 Jalan, Bimal, 2005, *The Future of India: Politics, Economics and Governance*, Viking/Penguin.
4 Halpern, David, 2015, *Inside the Nudge Unit: How Small Changes Can Make a Big Difference*, W.H. Allen.
5 Halpern, 2015, Ibid.
6 Ariely, Dan, 2012/2013, *The Honest Truth About Dishonesty: How We Lie to Everyone—Especially Ourselves*, Harper Collins, ebook.
7 Sunstein, Cass R., 2013, *Simpler: The Future of Government*, Simon and Schuster ebook.
8 Sunstein, Cass R., 2013, Ibid.

# 13

## Ease of Doing Business
### Licence-Permit Raj

Basic public services, the subject of Chapter 12, involve direct interactions between the government agent and the citizen. The logic and rationale of licencing, registration and approvals which concerns business and trade is to ensure that interests of the second party to a market exchange— consumers and customers—are protected. The objective of some of these regulations is also the welfare and health of the employees. Akerlof[1] et al. refer to the first food regulation of the meat packing houses in the USA, which was initiated when Upton Sinclair (*The Jungle*) exposed their unhygienic conditions. The regulations now extend to areas far beyond the essential contingencies mentioned by Akerlof, from nuclear plants to street hawkers and street walkers. In India, licencing and registration is required for manufacturing (practically all the manufacturing units are covered) drugs, food, oils, sugar, weights and measures, elementary schools as well as higher education (though the mid category, class 9 to 12, has been surprisingly left out!) As mentioned in *Introduction*, views on the desirability of economic and social regulations tend to be arrayed on the two extremes. Milton Friedman[2] was opposed to any type of regulation. On the other hand, Akerlof et al. justify[3] regulation in the interest of customers who may otherwise be easily manipulated. Whether any intervention is necessary probably depends on the context of a particular regulation or business. An astrophysicist in a TV show remarked that when the cyanobacteria appeared on our planet over 2 billion years ago, they made life difficult for the anaerobic creatures for whom oxygen was toxic; a government of the anaerobes, had there been one, would have put oxygen under a regulatory agency!

## Rationale for regulating business and trade

Sunstein[4] mentions that generally the Precautionary or Harm Principle is invoked for justifying such regulations — government should intervene if the behaviour and actions of an individual or a group puts others' welfare in jeopardy. Simply invoking this principle, however, is not enough and Sunstein rightly emphasises the need for carefully looking into the feasibility of a regulation as well as the costs and benefits thereof; a regulation must not impose net costs nor should we be satisfied with marginal benefits, as may be vaguely projected, without careful analysis. The *Paper Work Reduction Act* in the US seeks to ensure that regulations are not multiplied mindlessly just because that is the obvious thing bureaucrats know how to do.

## Problem of information asymmetry

The purpose of such regulations is to ensure that a business or a school or a factory delivers its outputs and services without inflicting damage or harm on others—by the sale of substandard or underweight goods, poor education, risky boilers and so on. The problem of hidden information, however, limits their effectiveness; information may not be available to the inspecting officials. Information about the production systems, infrastructure and machinery is mostly hidden and is now so complex and technologically advanced that it is difficult for government officials even to keep up with the knowledge. Short therefore of the equipment available to Big Brother (George Orwell's *Nineteen Eighty Four*), there is no way that the *ex ante* processes of licencing, regulation and approval can ensure that the objectives are achieved.

## Regulate performance, not process

In these cases, as Sunstein observes[5] government should lay down the *standards of performance rather than processes and systems for operation/manufacture of products and services.* Persons who adulterate drugs, mix urea in milk and so on are unlikely to go through the expensive processes of licencing and so on. Probably, except for drugs, nuclear plants and high rise buildings, where the design of equipment may be itself an indicator of performance and a free hand my involve high risks, the requirement of *prior* licencing, registration and approvals can be done away with.

## Nudging by 'Naming and Shaming'

In areas such as environment regulations, the strategies of 'naming and shaming' may be quick effective. Information can be used as a 'nudge' as has been demonstrated in US where the department publishes data on toxic releases by manufactures; information made available to the public through the *Toxic Release Inventory* has been sufficient to ensure better compliance by the manufacturers even in the absence of penalties and punishments for violation of the norms of omissions.

Economists refer to 'market failure' caused by externalities, monopolies and information asymmetry. In the case of most of the regulations for licencing and approvals, the problem of hidden information or information asymmetry makes governance failure inevitable. It may be desirable for governments to fix standards for performance rather than processes and where feasible, adopt the soft touch 'naming and shaming' in place of or in addition to penal provisions.

## Endnotes

1 Akerlof, A. and Schiller, Robert J., 2015, *Phishing for Phools: The Economic of Manipulation and Deception*, Princeton University Press.
2 Friedman, Milton and Friedman, Rose, 1980/1990, *Free to Choose*, Harvest Books/Harcourt.
3 Akerlof, A. and Schiller, Robert J., 2015, Ibid.
4 Sunstein, Cass R., 2013, *Simpler: The Future of Government*, Simon and Schuster ebook.
5 Sunstein, 2013, Ibid.

# 14

## Governance
### By Experts or Algorithms?

A business cannot develop 'core competency' in everything it does and the private sector is known for engaging and consulting experts not only for planning and construction of projects but also for operations. In India, this option is especially attractive due to labour laws and outsourcing has now extended beyond planning, design and critical components needing expert inputs, to routine but specialised operations such as housekeeping and accounting. The Central and State Governments are also finding it easier to market projects and proposals supported by expert advice as public have little faith in the objectivity and efficiency of officials, however well qualified. Moreover, unlike private sector organizations which are functionally more integrated, government departments and agencies have disparate divisions—finance, audit, purchase and so on—which may have lateral loyalties and affiliations; and the agencies also need to consult other departments. Decision making is therefore somewhat diffuse. The problem is complicated by the traditional tendering processes, where the lowest cost tender is generally the only risk free option for those who decide—an individual or a committee. Governments therefore find comfort in creating layers of outside experts and consultancies for pre-feasibility and feasibility reports, designing the contract documents, advising on the award of a project and even monitoring the progress thereof.

## Is experts' opinion reliable?

Philip Tetlock in a classic 2005 study[1] analyzed more than 80000 predictions made by experts and concluded that they performed worse than they would have if they had simply assigned equal probability to each of the three possible outcomes they were asked to choose from. As the book *The Wisdom of Crowds* demonstrates and as an analysis of TV shows such as *Kaun Banega Crorepati* indicates, *audience polls are much more reliable them expert opinion.* This does not mean that experts do not matter or that governments can afford to do without them. In fact in his latest book *Superforecasting,* Tetlock himself explores this aspect. It is difficult for example to see how the government could devise effective fiscal and monetary policy without the help of experts. What is argued here is just that in *some of the* areas of public policy, we may do well to work out appropriate algorithms, checklists or formulas in place of elaborate and complicated policy interventions devised by experts.

## Why algorithms matter?

Psychologists sometimes differentiate between heuristics and algorithms. Heuristics, as indicated in *Introduction* are thumb-rules devised by the intuitive and impulsive System I, or the 'hare brain' of the humans, for making choices, decisions and judgements. Stereotype of race, colour and religion for example is a heuristic. Algorithms are also simple rules of the thumb; the major difference is that they are logical and are devised by the deliberative System 2, or the 'tortoise mind' to help humans make correct decisions quickly.

Simple formulas and algorithms—digital, statistical or plain common sense—can many a time be much more useful than in-depth analyses and recommendations made by experts. Such algorithms have been widely adopted in many areas such as "diagnosis of cardiac disease, evaluation of credit risks by banks, prospects of success of new businesses"[2]. In public governance, however, we still go by complicated assessments, evaluations and recommendations made by teams of experts and consultants who may not necessarily follow the principle of Occam's razor, that entities should not be multiplied unnecessarily, whether for intervention or debate.

There are three areas where algorithms may be especially valuable and effective. One of these is the emergency situations where this is the only viable option. A medical emergency for example may not provide enough time for professionals to choose a particular course of action. That is the reason cardiac emergency units have simple triage systems to identify cases which need immediate attention. Similarly in the case for fire fighting, a quick decision is required to be made regarding the nature of the fire—chemical or LPG and so on. The knowledge even of experts in most of the areas is rarely perfect. Even specialists can differ regarding the diagnosis of a disease or symptom. Kahneman gives the example of Dr. Apgar who came up in the 1950s with a simple algorithm based on three variables, for new-borns with breathing problems; this algorithm could be used even by a nurse to identity serious cases and thus save babies who might otherwise die.

Algorithms can be useful even in common situations involving choice and selection of interventions, regulations, preferences and persons. One couldn't do better than refer to Kahneman regarding the utility of algorithms in decision making. As he puts it in a chapter *Intuitions vs*

*Formulas:* "The research suggests a surprising conclusion: to maximize predictive accuracy, final decision should be left to formulas or statistical predictions"[3].

## Basic public services

Many areas in public governance can benefit by the use of formulas and protocols. Delivery of basic public services is one area where, as suggested in Chapter 12, simple protocols or checklists for self certification can be blindly followed by officials without setting up a moral hazard or increasing the risk of misuse. Self certification is also adequate for most of the conventional areas of licencing and registration, for reasons given in Chapter 13. In fact online services cannot function without such algorithms. In the case of police verification for the issue of a passport, for example, the present police practice is to obtain statements of neighbours about the 'character' and 'respectability' of the applicant. And the applicant herself is supposed to procure these statements while the visiting policeman is sipping tea. The rules could instead provide that the police need only verify the place of residence. Information on whether the applicant has been convicted of any offence is available at the police station from the *National Criminal Tracking Network*. A simple checklist regarding residence and the record of conviction of the applicant will save the time and resources of the applicant, the neighbours and of course the police, especially when, as in States like Punjab, every adult may be applying for a passport sometime or the other!

## Institution of face-to-face interviews

Another area where algorithms can be very useful and save governments a lot of resources of money and time is that of recruitment of employees. Kahneman[4] gives the example of his experience in interviewing recruits for the army in Israel. A simple points system based on a candidate's replies to five questions was more effective than detailed and in depth interviews and assessments by qualified psychologists who devoted 15-30 minutes to each candidate. And probably that information could even be obtained without a face to face interview. Richard Nisbett refers to the 'interview illusion' caused by our judgement of the suitability of a candidate based on a single observation of behaviour, attitudes and traits of a candidate: "predictions based on the half-hour interview have been shown to correlate less than .10 with performance ratings of undergraduate and graduate students, as well as with performance ratings for army officers, businesspeople, medical students, Peace Corps volunteers, and every other category of people that has every been examined"[5].

Government is a major employer in India but there is a substantial lag in selections mainly due to the institution of personal interviews. Take for example the recruitment of policemen/army recruits. There are thousands of applicants for a limited number of jobs. Sometimes crowds of applicants have to be dispersed by force. The departments could develop algorithms based on the standards of physical fitness (height, chest and physical endurance) and academic performance, assign equal weight to these factors and make the selection. Needless to say, algorithms have to be based on verifiable facts and evidence, with little scope for opinion, especially when hundreds of candidates are to be recruited.

The GoI has recently announced that the institution of interviews will be discontinued for most of the posts. While the decision is a good innovation, it is likely to be confined to the basic entry level posts of peons, clerks etc. What the governments need to do is to develop simple formulas for selection and extend formula based selection processes right upto the middle level managers and professionals. It is difficult to break the bastions of belief in the sanctity of interviews for the recruitment of professionals and specialists whereas such protocols are likely to be much more useful precisely for these jobs. Interviews for a mass of recruits such as policemen or clerks do not provide much scope in any case for the expression of personal opinion or preference of the selection board members, except may be for reasons of favouritism or corruption; they simply don't have enough time for each candidate. Much more damage however can be caused by the biases of experts in the recruitment of professionals and managers; they have enough time to allow full expression to their behavioural biases—'halo' effect (a particular attribute of a candidate may crowd out all other traits and qualities to be considered); personal liking, the first impression of a candidate and various related problems associated with System 1, which constructs a simple coherent narrative of a candidate's ability and capability in the face of a large number of complex and uncertain factors which need to be considered but cannot be properly assessed during the interview.

Add to that the problem of 'group think'[6] which is very likely when four or five persons need to jointly decide on a particular candidate's suitability not *qua* that candidate but in comparison with many others who precede or may follow him/her. And then there are the stereotype biases—of gender, caste, state of domicile and so on—which may affect the judgement of those who make the selections. The members of the UPSC, the central selection body in India and the State Commissions will, however, not be rendered redundant; they can spend time more productively in developing algorithms for different posts and ranking candidates on that basis.

# Information disclosure: 'priming' the rule-makers

Mandatory information systems under the Right to Information ACT (RTI) would also do well with some assist from simple protocols. As remarked in *Governance Unbound*, the RTI rules provide a laid back and lazy solution to the disclosure of information, leaving it to the departments to understand the spirit and make proper disclosures, thus invoking the 'least effort principle' of the collective cognitive System 2 of a department.

I had given two such formats for disclosure of information in *Governance Unbound*. The RTI Rules could provide budget expenses, for example, to be displayed in the following format:

**Information Disclosure 'Module':**
**Budget and Expenditure under Section 4(1)(b)**

| 1<br>Budget items/schemes | 2<br>Estimates<br>current year | 3<br>Actuals<br>previous year |
|---|---|---|
| Total budget of the department/ agency | | |
| Total staff salaries and staff related expenditure | | |
| Total non staff budget (capital) (Rs.) | | |
| Details of non staff expenditure (all items more than Rs. 10 lakhs) | | |
| (a) Capital | | |
| (i) | | |
| (ii) | | |
| (b) Revenue | | |
| (i) | | |
| (ii) | | |

Similarly, information on purchase of goods and services and contracts could be prescribed by the rules to be displayed in the following format:

**Information Disclosure 'Module' — Contracts/Purchases**

| Description of purchase/ contract | Estimated cost | Details of bidders and price quoted | Contract price and party selected | Date of final payment |
|---|---|---|---|---|
| | | | | |

*Note:*

(i) Information must be displayed on the website up to six months from the date of final payment.

(ii) Information must be displayed within one month of the award of the contract of purchase and updated monthly.

Such modules will function as 'channel factors' which have been defined as 'small influences that could either facilitate or prohibit certain behaviours'.[7] *The only difference is that priming in this case is required not for the public, but for the government agents responsible for displaying information. What better way to prime bureaucrats than the rules they themselves swear by!*

## Market matching algorithms

There are a number of areas which are today loosely and somewhat chaotically regulated by the government or public entities and where the principles of market design may be helpful. Alvin E. Roth who has contributed substantially in many areas of public policy by providing market matching algorithms observes "A market involves matching whenever price isn't the only determinant of who gets what"[8]. The National Residents Matching Programme is a clearing house for matching Resident doctors and hospitals all over the US. Similarly computer algorithms have been developed for school admissions in many school districts in the USA. I have mentioned in Chapter 1 the desirability of adopting or developing the kidney matching algorithms for donors and recipients in India.

The confusing and multiple systems of student admissions in schools under the RTE (Right to Education) Act (separate applications for each school and separate queues), and in the medical/engineering institutions, impose tremendous and unnecessary social costs. It is a pity that barring the IIT's and the IIMs, these socio economic markets are allowed to be so chaotic and wasteful both for the students and the educational institutions. We could use some of the matching algorithms evolved in the US by Roth and other experts and impose some order in these chaotic markets. Needless to say algorithms in these areas are complex and may require expert inputs; there are some areas where one may need experts after all! System I is well equipped to respond to such mechanisms and as Atul Gawande shows[9], even professionals need to be nudged by them.

## Endnotes

1 Tetlock, Philip, 2005, *Expert Political Judgement: How Good Is It? How Can We Know?*

2 Kahneman, Daniel, 2011, *Thinking Fast & Slow,* Farrar, Straus & Giroux, New York.

3 Kahneman, 2011, Ibid.

4 Ibid.

5 Nisbett, Richard E., 2015, *Mindware: Tools for Smart Thinking*, Allen Lane, p. 117.

6 Janis, Irving, 1983, *Group Think,* 2nd revised edition, Houghton Mifflin, Boston.

7 Thaler and Sunstein, 2008, Ibid, Quoting Kurt Lewis.

8 Roth, Alvin E., 2015, *Who Gets What And Why,* William Harper Collins, Indian Edition.

9 Gawande, Atul 2010/2011, *The Checklist Manifesto,* Penguin Books.

# 15

# Redesigning Rules of the Game
## From Noise to Cooperation

The new paradigm of governance came into public discourse in the 1990s but it does not appear to have disturbed the stable equilibrium of the governmental processes, institutions or outcomes in India[1]. The state of public governance in India painted by books, surveys or opinion polls remains dismal. Views of the outsiders[2] and the insiders[3] are no different; *The Rogue Elephant* has depressing chapter headings like *"Hell is for Children"*, *'Whistle blowers under attack in India's Bureaucracy'*. One is tempted to attribute governance failure to a lack of Putnam's 'social capital'[4], the trust and consideration for others in the Indian society. My own belief is that most of our behaviour is contextual. Even persons who are good Samaritans by profession and training did not stop to help an accident victim (of course a fake and a confederate of the experimenter) when 'primed' that they were late for an urgent appointment. We simply extend the 'fundamental attribution error'—the common human tendency to attribute behaviour and actions to the main disposition of individuals rather than the situation—from individuals who may be 'bowling alone' to stereotype whole communities. Whether Indian have or lack social capital, it is generally agreed that there is little of what I call 'governance capital; there is just no good will for or trust in government—in Putnam's words, little of 'bonding' within the government and less of 'bridging' between the government and the society. Most of the policies, therefore, which ultimately depend on citizen cooperation, tend to fail. This chapter deals with some meta aspects of the rule design necessary for building governance capital: avoid making noisy rules and have instead rules which encourage, as a general principle, cooperation rather than confrontation.

## Noisy rules: some examples

White noise refers to the static in the TV sets and the term noise trader is used in the share markets to refer to an inexperienced novice who follows the herd; he is the last person who is left stranded and therefore suffers the most—no chair is left for him in this game of musical chairs. By 'noisy' rules I mean the rules which have little rationale or logic and play no role at all in influencing behaviour and actions; the rules are just there because somebody happened to design them and we are too lazy to review them. 'Noise traders' end up harming themselves but noisy governance rules are a social burden which impose costs both on the public agency that administers them and the citizens who need to comply with them.

## Rules for registration of births

My favourite example is drawn from the *Birth and Death Registration Act* in India. Over 30 years ago a new provision was introduced that a birth will not be registered, if reported 15 years after the event. Probably the logic was to apply some coercive pressure on the laggard families who failed to report the event of birth even within 15 years. What, however, the law ends up doing is to penalise a person for the sins of omission of the parents! I came across a similar example a few years ago, through a news report, which I have been unable to trace. This was about a rule made by a state government to discourage child marriages. Obviously a child marriage involves minors but the rule provided that the bride as well as the bridegroom would be barred from government employment!

## Security check at airports

I had given another instance of a noisy rule in *Governance Unbound*. Airport security regulations in India require that each and every hand luggage as well as the boarding card of the passengers must be stamped to provide proof of security clearance and the same is checked before boarding—a pointless ritual unique to India.

## Licences, permissions and renewals

Another example is the institution of various licences and approvals—driving, guns, passports which need to be renewed periodically. One can ignore the basic problem of bogus driving licences issued to unqualified candidates who could pay a bribe as a study[5] showed, but even the minor mechanics of renewal of a driving licence can put the public in trouble. For persons of +45 years, the renewal is limited to five years at a time. For the driver of a heavy vehicle, renewal is required every three years irrespective of age. There seems little logic or rationale behind this regulation. What is the point of making the licence valid for 3 or 5 years; why not for life or, say, for 20 years, in both cases? Similar is the case for the grant of a certificate of fitness for commercial vehicles; this is required to be renewed every year. As a colleague in government, who started a transport agency after retirement and was understandably bitter about such whimsical regulations, told me, the contingency of a commercial vehicle becoming unfit could occur any day and the government should ideally require commercial vehicles to get a fitness certificate every day!

## Labour wages: payable in hard cash

Section 6 of the *Payment of Wages Act* 1936 provides that all wages shall be paid in current coin or currency notes or both. I came to know of this somewhat mysterious clause in the 1980's when major projects in Punjab, having huge labour on their rolls, were struggling with the problem of cashiers being robbed on way to places of disbursement of labour wages. It turned out that giving a cheque was illegal! Some states have amended this section to provide for payment of bonus etc. by cheque, but otherwise the rule is operative even till today. It does create a noisy jingle!

## Fire safety regulations

Take the case of a certificate of fire safety for multi-storey buildings. In Chandigarh, the regulations cover even commercial buildings having only three floors which may not even have lifts but these require the owners to install smoke detection equipment and automatic spray systems all of which can cost upto 5% of the project. The common practice is to put up dummy equipment and get the approval. On the other hand, multi storeye flats developed by 'fly by night' operators manage to side step even elementary safety measures. I know of an instance where the purchaser of a flat in a high rise complex discovered that bare electricity wires had been laid within the walls without any conduit protection; and of course the developer had secured all the clearances. Such rules simply add to transaction costs without necessarily ensuring compliance.

## Cooperation, collusion and retribution

The issue whether cooperation is—genetically driven—a process of 'kin selection'—or an outcome of the process of socialization—'reciprocal altruism' is not finally settled; governments, however, need not wait for the final verdict.

In Chapter 6, I have referred to a study by Brosnan Sarah and Frans BM de Waad (*"Monkeys reject equal pay"*; Nature 428, 140, March 2004), where capuchin monkeys were paired up and trained to surrender a token in order to receive a reward of cucumber slices. The subject monkey resented the discrimination when another monkey was given a more desirable reward, grapes: this behaviour is "an early evolutionary origin of inequity aversion" or the 'fairness gene'[6]. We have the Ultimatum game where a participant A may reject the offer of $10 he would get gratis if he accepts B's offer to share $100 in the ratio of 90:10 (with $90 of course going into the pocket of 'B'). Evidently, as it shows, *humans value fairness even though it may result in a personal loss;* making B suffer the loss of $90 is sweet revenge.

## Public goods and cooperation

In the case of public goods, such as vaccination or judicious use of antibiotics, governments need citizens to cooperate. Each child needs to be administered the polio vaccine as even one child who is not inoculated can jeopardise the health of whole populations. Over-use of antibiotics may or may not help the patient but can expose many others to pain, suffering or extra expense on expensive antibiotics which may not even be helpful to the patient. A traditional carrot and stick regime in these situations—punishing parents if the child is not enrolled in school, penalty for the person who fails to get inoculated—is not very relevant.

Thanks to the influence of the WHO and others, we are now shifting from a regime of punitive to cooperative rules, as shown by the success of the polio vaccination programme. Instead of exhorting people to take babies to clinics, the health staff started providing vaccination right at the door-step. Similar is the case with the handling of accident cases. In India, people would rarely report a crime or even an accident or take the injured to the hospital in the case of a road accident, due to the fear of harassment by the police. Even in tl ɘ West, which is believed to have a more socially oriented citizenry, there is the famous 1964 case of murder of Kitty Genovese in New York; over thirty eight persons witnessed her being stabbed to death but none of them called the police. This is attributed to 'bystander apathy'—you don't report a crime because you feel somebody else is bound to report, or in the case of an accident, to stop and transport the injured to the hospital. Even at the risk of possible misuse in some cases, we need to provide immunity to the altruistic bystander who chooses to intervene.

On the other hand, in the case of public 'bads', we need to encourage persons who may be party to collusive interactions, to become whistle blowers. One example is that of sex determination tests, as shown in Chapter 2. Similar is the case for anti corruption laws where bribe-givers can be encouraged to be the whistleblowers, though the applicability of the approach is limited, as indicated elsewhere.

## Misuse of central government funds: cheating a stranger is easy

It is well known that it is easier to cheat a stranger or a member of the out-group rather than a friend or a member of the in-group. Probably one major problem why there is so much leakage and waste in the government programmes in India is the multiple layers and filters between the Central Government which provides funds—for MNREGA, Food Security and so on, and the executive and 'street' levels at which the relevant exchanges and interactions take place. Steve Hilton has advocated[7] an aggressive strategy of 'radical localism' to promote policy outcomes. It may be a prudent policy for the central government to transfer funds for the core programmes to the states (or even to Panchayats) and give them autonomy in spending them. This financial *subsidiarity* may result in less of cheating, misuse and more local accountability, rather than layers of auditors and supervisors working on behalf of the remote principal, the Central Ministry. This not only multiplies manifold the agency problem but may be partly responsible for the flagrant misuse of funds; the central ministry is the outgroup, the 'other'.

## Designing institutions for cooperative behaviour

The State has devised various rules and institutions of interaction been trying to get citizens to cooperate, not only among themselves—by punishing aberrations like personal violence and breach of trust—but also with the State agencies—in paying, rather than evading taxes for example. Unfortunately, little weight or consideration is given to the factors of behaviour, motives and incentives of actors—government and private—while designing 'rules of the game' for various public services and regulations. The micro, operational and interactional rules of governance need to be designed to encourage (or otherwise) cooperation and compliance to achieve the objectives desired rather than, as they seem to do at present, encouraging collusion and perverse incentives. And for this we don't require *deux ex machina* but rather the humble instrument of the operational rules and institutions.

One simple design principle is to make it convenient and easy for people to comply. It has been seen for example that people cooperate in garbage management if garbage collection centres are conveniently located. Similarly carbon credits/trading is one way to make compliance with the emissions norms for sulphurous gases easier. Utilities may agree to spend more money on buying credits for generating pollution rather than face imprisonment or heavy fines. If the penalty, however, is very harsh—say life imprisonment for a polluter—industry is likely to devise strategies to evade rather than comply.

Governments need to keep in view that just because a rule or law is placed on the statute books does not mean that it will be complied with. Petty thefts continued even when the punishment was very severe—chopping off one limb or the other. It may be desirable to have rules which are sensible and rational and encourage compliance through cooperation rather than confrontation.

## Endnotes

1 Please see Gupta, R.N., *Governance Unbound*, Chapter 2.
2 Denver, Simon, Bloomsbury, 2014, *The Rogue Elephant: Harnessing the Power of India's Unruly Democracy.*
3 M. Godbole an insider, has given an evocative title to his book *Good Governance: Never on India's Radar,* 2014, Rupa Publications, New Delhi.
4 Putnam, David Robert, 2000, *Bowling Alone: The Collapse and Revival of the American Community*, New York: Simon & Schuster.
5 Marianne B., Djankov, Simeon, Henna, Rema, Mullainathan, Sendhil, 2007, 'Obtaining a Driving Licence in India; An Experimental Approach to Studying Corruption', *Quarterly Journal of Economics*, November, 1639–1676.
6 Linklater, Andro, 2014, *Owning The Earth: The Transforming History of Land Ownership*, Bloomsbury.
7 Hilton, Steve, 2015, *More Human: Designing A World Where People Come First*; WH Allen, UK.

# Index

affidavits, 123–125,
  cost of, 124
Akerlof, A, 69, 130,
  *Phishing for Phools*, 4
alcohol: 56–58
and maturity, 57
and standardisation, 57
algorithms, 135–136
and market matching, 141–2
and school admissions, 141
and interviews, 137–9
Alvin, Roth E, 20, 22,
  *Who Gets What And Why*, 141
anchor, 62
ANM, 5
antibiotics, 147
Apgar, Dr., 136
Ariely , Dan, 75, 127,
  *Predictably Irrational*, 5
Asch, Golman, 8
ASHA, 5
Axelrod, Robert, 83

Balri Rakshak Yojana, 29
Banerjee, Abhijit, 12/n
Basic services, 123–6
  and transaction cost, 125–6
  and verification process,
  123–124

Basu, Kaushik, 11, 94/n
behavioural governance failure,
  10, 30
Behavioural Insights Team, (xi)
behaviourally informed approach,
  (x), 3, 26, 27
Behaviourism, (xi)
Bernoulli, Daniel, 70
big ticket corruption, 90
bonding, 143
Bridging, 143
Broken windows, 70, 90
Brosnan, Sarah, 109, 147
bureaucracy: 95–102
  and fairness in punishment,
  98–9
  and fairness in rewards, 95
  and assessment of performance,
  106–7
  and incentives, 105–6
bystander apathy, 148

Capuchin monkeys experiment,
  147
Carney, Scott, 13, *The Red Market*, 22
Cassidy, John, 11/n
CBI, 93
Central Government funds, misuse
  of, 148–9

Central Registration System, 23
Central Secretariat Manual,
    Government of India, 111
Channel factors, 141
child sex ratio, 23
choice architect, choice architecture,
    5
Cialdini, Robert B, 4
cigarette smoking, 88
clinical practices, 24
cognitive dissonance, 112
compounding of offences, 81–2
cooperation, 159
    and public goods, 147–8
corruption, 85–88
    and disproportionate assets,
        86–7
    and integrity codes, 87–8
    and lavish consumption, 86–7
    and civil service pay, 85–6
        in Uganda, 88
        in Indonesia, 88
CPIB, 89
crime in USA, 75
cyanobacteria, 131

Dan, Daniel M, 22
de Waad, Frans BM, 109
death duties, 70–71
default list of organs 19–20
default rules, 7
Default rule for compounding
    offences, 81
Denver, Simon, 143 (n)
Diamond, Jared, 80
DNA, 8
donation of organs, 14–18
by relatives, 14–5
    and timing, 18–9
    and matching compatibility, 20
Dreze, Jean, 24, 34
Driving licence renewal, 145

Duflo, Esther, 12/n

Econ, 8
Edison, Thomas, 75
Einstein, Albert, (ii)
Eyesenck, 56

fairness gene, 147
female foeticide, 23–4
    and emotional factors, 27
    and economic incentives, 28
    and incentives of service
        providers, 28/29
FIR, 77–9
report and registration, 77–8
free-rider problem, 26
Friedman, Milton, 2, 130
fundamental attribution error, 143

Galbraith, John Kenneth, 2
garbage management, 159
Gawande, Atul, 142,
    *Checklist Manifesto*, 142
Gladwell, Malcolm, (x), 60, 79, 100,
    *The Tipping Point* (x)
Gneezy, Uri, 11/n, 22
Godbole, M, 160(n)
governance capital, 143
group think, 113, 139
Gupta, R.N., 129,
*Governance Unbound*, (xii), 8

halo effect, 139
Halpern, David, 9, 50, 59, 62, 129
happiness index, 33
hare brain, 135
Harford, Tim, 75
harvesting of organs, 16–7
heuristics and biases, 3
heuristics and algorithms, 135
Hilton, Steve, 2
Homo economicus, 112

Hongkong, 88–9
human centred design, 7
hyperbolic discounting, 29, 63

ICAC, 89
IIMs, 142
IITs, 142
Indhradhanush vaccination
    programme, 23
Indian Factories Act 1988, 114
inequity aversion, 147
information asymmetry, 131–2
information disclosure, 139–140
    and budget, 140
informational cascade, 126
Intention – implementation gap, 6
Invisible foot strategy, 31, 34
invisible hand, 32
Iran, 21
Irving, Janis, 113,
    *Group Think*, 113/n, 139
ISEP, 99

Kahneman, Daniel, 70, 136
Kaw, M.K., 108
Konnikova, Maria, 3

Labour law reforms, 114–119
    and forms, registers and returns,
    117–119
Lambsdorff, Johann Graf, 35
law of small numbers, 30
licencing of factories, 116
Link later, Andro, 160/n
List, John, 11/n
Lokpal Act, 92
loose cigarette sales, 52–3
loss aversion, 62
Lotte Jr. John, 75
lottery for pregnant women, 32–4
low alcohol drinks, 58–9

Malimath Committee Report, 72–4
mandated choice, 17–18
market failure, 132–3
marshmellow studies, 29
matching algorithms, 20–21
micro governance, 2
minimum government, 1
minimum wages, 119–120
monkey on the shoulder, 4
moral hazard in girl-child
    promotion schemes, 29
MTP Act, 25

Naidu, PR Ramdas, 77
Naming and shaming, 31, 132
National Pension Scheme, 64
National residents matching
    programme, USA, 141
NFHS, 24
nicotine chewing gum, 52
NIH bias, 74–75
*Nineteen eighty four*, 132
NIPFP, 65
Nisbett, Richard E, 4, 10
noise traders, 144
noisy rules, 144
Norman, Don, 7
North, Douglass, 6
NPM, 1

OIRA, (iii)
Olson, Mancur, 100
Option overload, 98
Orwell, George, 132
Over confidence bias, 75, 107
    Panchayats, 30
Paper Work Reduction Act USA,
    131
Passport verification, 137
Payment of Wages Act, 146
PCPNDT Act 23, 93

Performance pay, 108–9
Phishing equilibrium, 69
Piketty, Thomas, 71
Pinker, Steven, 82
Polio, 147
pragmatic reasoning schemas, 10
precautionary principle, 131
presumed consent, 17–18
presumptive tax, 64–5
Prevention of Corruption Act, 85–6
priming, 139, 140
prisoner's dilemma, 83
process and performance, 132
procrastination and smoking, 51
proportionality principle, 32
public donors, 15–16
public goods and cooperation, 147–8
public health, 147
Punishment and Appeal Rules, 101
purchases and contracts, 141
Putnam, Daniel Robert, 143

radical localism, 149
rational actor model, 4
RCTs, 9–10
Reagan, Ronald, 1
Registration of Birth and Death Act, 5, 144
Report on Presumptive Direct Taxation, 65
Ridley, Matt, (iii)
Ramalingam Ben, 74
Roosevelt, Theodore, 59
Roth, Alvin E., 20, 22
RTE Act, 142
rules of the game, 6
rule 80:20, 90

Sample Registration System, 23
scared straight programmes, 9
Security check airports, 145

self certification, 125–6
self declaration, 124–6
self interest, 4
Sen, Amartya, 24/34
Sex ratio at birth, 23
sex ratio, 23
Sharma, Mihir, 114
Sherlock Holmes system, 3
Sherman, Michael, 27, 35
Simplification of forms, 127–8
Sinclair, Upton, 130
Singapore, 88–89
Size of bottles and servings, 58
Smith, Adam, 2
Smoker's personality, 56
Smoking – prices and taxes, 50–1
    in public places, 50
    and substitutes, 51–2
    and social proof, 62
social capital, 143
social cost of regulations, 24
social environment, 6
social Epidemic, (ii)
Social norms marketing, 54–5, 71
Soman, Dilip, 11/n, *The Last Mile*, 2
SOP's, 111
Stanford University, 29
sticky message, 68–69
street level bureaucracy
student loan applications USA, 128
subsidiarty, 149
Sunstein , Cass R, (iii), (iv), 8, 60, 129 131, 133/n
Surowiecki, James, 113,
    *The Wisdom of Crowds*, 135
System 1, 3, 5, 8, 51, 135
System 2, 3, 8, 51, 135

tax base, 65–66
tax proposals budget 2016–17, 63–4
tax returns, 66
and turnover, 67

and tax payment, 68
Ten Commandments, 88
Tetlock, Philip, 135
Thaler, Richard, 17, *Nudge*, x
The Economist, (x), 49/n
*The Rogue Elephant*, 143
theory of everything, (x)
Titmuss, Richard M, 13, 34
tortoise mind, 135
Toxic Release Inventory, USA, 132
tragedy of the commons, 34
Transfers in bureaucracy, 100
Transparency international, 72
Transplantation of Human Organs and Tissues Act 1994, 13
Tversky, Ames, (x)
Tylor, Edward, 27

Ultimatum game, 147
UPSC, 139

VAT, 67

Wade, Nicholas, 35
Wade, Robert, 100
Watson System, 3
Watson, John B. (xi)
wealth tax, 70–1
white noise, 144
Wilson, James Q, 74, 75, 76, 90, 109
World Bank, 72

zarda consumers, 54
zero FIR, 79
zero tolerance, 89–90